THE *POWER* OF
NO

THE *POWER* OF

NO

*How to Keep Blowhards
and Bozos at Bay*

BETH WAREHAM

RODALE

Rodale books may be purchased for business or promotional use or for special sales. For information, please write to:
Special Markets Department, Rodale Inc., 733 Third Avenue, New York, NY 10017

Printed in the United States of America
Rodale Inc. makes every effort to use acid-free ♾, recycled paper ♻.

Illustrations by Carolita Johnson
Book design by Anthony Serge

Library of Congress Cataloging-in-Publication Data

Wareham, Beth.
  The power of no : how to keep blowhards and bozos at bay / Beth Wareham.
      p.   cm.
  Includes index.
  ISBN-13 978–1–59486–650–0   hardcover
  ISBN-10 1–59486–650–3   hardcover
  1. Interpersonal relations.   2. Interpersonal conflict.   I. Title.
  HM1106.W363   2009
158.2—dc22   2008040864

Distributed to the trade by Macmillan

2   4   6   8   10   9   7   5   3   1   hardcover

We inspire and enable people to improve their lives and the world around them

For more of our products visit **rodalestore.com** or call 800-848-4735

To Bernie,
the man I no best

Elegance is innate. It has nothing to do with being well dressed. Elegance is refusal.

Diana Vreeland

CONTENTS

INTRODUCTION

NOW, MORE THAN EVER

Why no now? Because we are under siege. Everything is blinking and beeping and buzzing and saying "Look at me!" "Listen to me!" "Buy me!" "Lease Me!" Endless e-mail blasts sell tires and gel inserts on the same machine you tell your mate your most intimate thoughts. Mass cell-phone texts say things like "Carlos has changed his number to 917-555-9060 and hopes to hear from you soon." Who the hell is Carlos, and why did he change his number? And what does that have to do with me? Was Carlos my boyfriend and I forgot? Was he my accountant, a person I should never forget? The question haunts me for several weeks. Then one day while I'm eating a huge platter of enchiladas for lunch, my middle-aged mind makes the "enchilada . . . Carlos . . . a trainer I once trained with" connection. But that was years ago! Dude, get outta my phone.

All the lines between private and professional have blurred. While you're at work thinking about a presentation, your computer vomits unsolicited Xanax and Viagra offers. While you have an important client on your cell phone, Mary Anne keeps beeping in to see if you can do a one-off and drive carpool in the morning. Your landline rings, and just as your favorite aunt says, "They've found something funny in my number two," the coffeepot starts beeping and UPS knocks.

Wow. No wonder you're in a bad mood.

Might I suggest that maybe you don't have too much to do; you have too many people and machines that want you to do something. "Drive my carpool!" "Turn the beeper off, the brewing is done!" "Spend an hour guessing what's in my number two!" "Sign this, please."

With so many "Can you do me this one little favor?" delivery devices, you must learn to be vigilant to time wasters, bliss stealers, and the generally tedious. For if you don't, your life will feel like that of an aging donkey stabled outside Basra. You will be exhausted, out of ideas, overloaded, and scared half to death.

But there is one little word that can keep you safe. . . .

MY NO CONVERSION

The terrible **yes years***—I remember them well. I spent the first half of my life saying yes to teachers, colleagues, bosses, boyfriends, strangers, acquaintances, girlfriends, and family mem-

*Boldface terms are defined in the Glossary on page 123.

bers. I thought that if I was a good enough girl, if I did what everyone wanted me to do at all times, not only would they love me, they would love me forever, not just *right now,* and life would flow smooth and be stress free. No fights. No cross-purposes. Great times.

Rather than say no, I spent countless evenings with people I didn't like. I wore clothes that had friends squealing in delight in the dressing room; I felt like a huge, pink Hostess snack every time I put it on. I was always the designated driver, the "Can you just swing by and pick me up some beer on the way?" girl. I ended up pretty mad at everyone all the time and, finally, enraged at myself. Oh, the horrors of yes.

> *You like me. Right now!*
> *You like me!*
> SALLY FIELD

Looking deeper, wincing the whole time, I understood that in my endless yessing, I was literally burning the days of my life up, my spirit ending up in little piles in other people's ashtrays. There was Robert, a man I spent three years with, in my prime. Three years right in the middle of the firm, high butt phase I diddled away on Robert. I spent $250 on baseball tickets (third base!), and Robert called me two hours before and told me he couldn't go. Robert took issue with the size of my thighs, a fact that tortured me then and now makes me giggle. (My thighs are a pair of curvaceous, muscular wonders that my husband calls the jaws of life.)

I mean, I dieted for Robert. Can it really get uglier than that?

It took a long time to say no to Robert. It took a lot of tears. I had known from the second week of dating that he was incapable of love, but my ego said, "I am going to make this guy love me." At that moment I was lost, chasing a yes that was not possible. Robert had one serious love, and that was Robert.

I don't believe in dieting.
JOAN COLLINS

The energy it took to disperse the thoughts *Well, maybe I am too emotional* and *Maybe I do always accuse him of ignoring me the week after we have sex* and *Maybe I should pay for everything because I make so much more money* and *Maybe I am a bit heavy* and *Maybe I need to learn to not be so impulsive* and *Maybe I do need too much attention* was profound. This guy had a kind of dog's nose for my old wounds and would paw them open at every turn. This guy was a pile of crap.

It took me three years to say no to Robert and another two to actually not feel him anymore. That's five years, or given the life expectancy for a North American female, one-fifteenth of my time on earth. The inability to say no suddenly felt a bit life threatening.

INTRODUCTION

Twenty-five years after I heard Robert say, "You could stand to lose a little here" as he pinched my thigh, I was crossing town fast on Forty-Eighth Street at noontime, already late for a Brazilian bikini wax, a strident form of yes that includes visions of my glorious thighs, glistening as they crash, hair free, through the frothy surf. All the way there, I was thinking about the word *no*. I marveled that I had to wait decades to use no frequently, with confidence, and to great effect. After all, if my baby book is to be believed, *no* was the first word out of my mouth. Unfortunately, that great verbal start soon faded, and I became mired in the terrible yes years. From age 15 to about 45, I was a yessing, people-pleasing weenie who might as well have had a sticky note on my back that said "kick me."

I spent the yes years not only thinking about men not worth a moment's thought but dating and agonizing over them for months, even years. Yes, I'll go out with you. Yes, I'll watch you change the oil in your car. Yes, your uncle can come to the game with us.

At work, it was just as bad. Yes, I did my job and half the job of the bimbo who was playing the boss. If there was late-night duty, I was willing and able. (I didn't want to get fired!) When colleagues with families fled at the first sign of snow, I worked on, single and therefore less likely to wreck a car in bad weather.

I was a publicist, one of the ugliest yes jobs in America. When I see television shows about the danger of trawling for king crab in the Arctic Ocean, I snicker. Yes, a 20-foot wave of icy sea water is scary, but have you ever been near a B-level actress when her limo didn't arrive? What exactly do you do when an author submits a bill for a private jet for $40,000 and you have only $10,000 in the budget? And—my personal favorite—whom do you call when your client has barricaded himself into a junior suite at the Four Seasons and drunkenly tells a *New York Times* reporter that he isn't coming down until Elvis arrives?

Being a publicist is a difficult, nuanced job that requires so much people pleasing at the expense of your own needs, most who do it need hospitalization after a while. You may find the following moments unbelievable, but they are all true. And if you ask any publicists you know to tell you stories, you will hear the same thing (or much worse if they work in LA).

I was cornered and excoriated at a huge symposium of colleagues by the author of *I Knew You Were Coming So I Baked a Cake* because I could not get her on a national morning television show. Her 100 recipes such as Make Me Late to Work Cake and Mama's Applesauce Glory Cake didn't catch the ear of the producer who had just booked O.J.'s old girlfriend. I had to call hundreds of news media to announce the first book on toilet training your cat. I had a cookbook author about to go on the Food Network call screaming because the fresh herbs brought by the food stylist were "not perky." I walked into my garden; pulled up a combination of catnip, mint, and weeds; chopped them up together; and sent it by messenger across town. This culinary expert never questioned the greens, used them on air, and called me later to rave about how great he was.

One author was on his way to a huge speaking engagement, got to the airport, saw his plane was delayed, and called his mother to come pick him up. He didn't wait for the next plane. He didn't call me or the presenters of the event. A 53-year-old man on his way to an important business meeting for a book published by a world-renowned company called his mommy and went back home.

I had an author show up wildly drunk at a bookstore for a reading. When he saw his name misspelled on a handmade sign, he trashed the place—broken shelves, piles of paperbacks on the floor. I had a client who wanted to stay in the closet yet endlessly announced "I am not gay" to any reporter who came near him. I took way too many calls at 3:00 a.m., posted too much bail, and spun so many sows' ears into silk purses that my relationship with reality was on the rocks.

In my late thirties—old for a publicist—I began to encounter the stuff that separates the girls from the women. My mother had breast cancer and was dying. My oldest brother would follow her three months later—just two days after the September 11 terrorist attacks a half mile from my front stoop. (See what an event like that does to your homeowner's insurance—talk about terrorism.) Grief jumped me and pummeled me for months, if not years.

Fine one moment, I would weep bitterly at a television

commercial the next. I cried over the cuteness of dogs in the streets and babies in strollers. I couldn't sleep, and I couldn't sit still. I would be walking, very old ladylike, down a sidewalk and suddenly begin gasping for air, and not a threatening, Goth-looking, studded-collar-wearing New York pit bull in sight. I got into such a bitter argument with the dry cleaner over a pair of black pants (albeit one half of a really, really expensive suit) that even I was appalled at the force of my emotion; I was crying and spitting at this tiny Korean man as if he had just said, "You can never have a peanut M&M again."

I had finally experienced "the fragility of life" up close and personal. I watched my mother take her last breath. I participated in the decision to take my brother off life support. I stood in front of all the flowers and cards and photos of the dead from 9/11 and completely lost it when I saw a subway wall that had been spray painted with "Dad, I came looking for you."

They were all gone, every one of them.

What, in the end, did it mean? I knew I wasn't supposed to curl into a ball and exist on pain and bag after bag of store-bought cookies. The point, finally, was living. It was all I could do, and if it was all I could do, I needed to do it well.

And that meant learning to say no.

First, I said no to the ugliest of yes jobs and left publicity to become a book editor. In one day, my job description changed from "mopping the pee off the floor" to "making decisions."

"Friends" who repeatedly cancelled on me ceased to be invited. If I saw them, fine, but I stopped seeking them out to make plans.

I changed my cell phone number and gave it only to family and friends. In the evenings and on weekends, if someone wanted to talk business, they could leave me a message at work, where the message belonged.

> *I feel like a human piñata.*
> *The disappointing thing is, no*
> *candy is going to spill out.*
> KATIE COURIC

I started paying off credit cards as fast as I could to quash the low hum of rapacious creditors who changed the due dates of bills, raised and lowered my maximum willy-nilly, and hit me with fees and penalties so often, I felt like a toothless forward on an ice hockey team.

And I told my husband that I would never unload the dishwasher again. It didn't matter how intense our game of chicken became—could the dishes sit in there for two days? Five days? A week?—it was his chore, and I would not do it.

From these small and large noes came something magical: more time for myself and the people I loved and the things I loved to do. I started skiing again and paid for it with cash. Instead of answering e-mails at day's end, I promised myself one hour in bed with a book every night—and not a book I needed to read for work, either. I refused myself those quickie shopping expeditions at lunch, took the money, and hired a trainer instead. I'd certainly look better in all the great clothes I already owned if I'd shake my booty a bit.

Saying no creates the time and space to live the life you want; it's the powerful tool that gets what you desire in this world. You've gotta get the noise out of your face and find the quiet to build the things you want to build. I've learned to say it in a multitude of ways that both flatter and offend. I say it with equal vigor at home, in the workplace, and out on the street. I use it to keep people out of my life and the people in my life reasonable and stable—at least when it comes to dealing with me. I use it for balance and dignity and, most important, as a way to protect who and what I am. I even no myself.

Each time I say no, I develop a little more courage and honesty. Recently, I said to a powerful book agent, "That's not the way I will do business." There was no "you said, I said," no accusations of lying or withholding the truth. I just wasn't going to do what I didn't want to do, no matter what the price. A week later she called me about a new project, and the negotiation was brief, respectful, and mutually beneficial.

I have told my husband that he cannot pretend to be deaf anymore, and by God, he now uses his third hand—the clicker—to mute the sound when I walk in the room and ask him a question. It is an amazing feeling to be consistently acknowledged by the man you love, and no got me there.

As I become more skilled at the many ways to deliver no, I also begin to know who is in my life for me and who is in my life for what they can get me to do. Big difference. I also get time—time that I can spend on something meaningful to me rather than something I didn't want to do in the first place.

I said no to managing a publicity department of young women whose tales of New York dating frightened and exhausted me. One woman was dating Chucky, and each day she would come in, terrorized and resentful, and proceed to yell at book reviewers all day on the phone. "You didn't like it?" she'd cry incredulously. "Did you read it to the end?" Another's boyfriend was gay, which was apparent to everyone but her, even when he endlessly listened to Liza Minnelli's version of "Send in the Clowns."

And there was my beloved Robin. She was so kind and steady and slyly funny, and she was completely dedicated to a young man who actually had her paged at an airport and, when she got to the JetBlue counter and picked up the red phone, said, "Don't get on the plane. I don't want to see you." He didn't know that before she got in the taxi to catch her flight? Yet Robin loved on, oblivious to the outraged voices of friends and family around her, all begging her to give this loser the boot.

I listened, cajoled, and tried to encourage these young women to make a stand, to say no and mean it. But then I realized the students were not ready; the teacher had not yet arrived. Those young women had years of painful yesses in front of them, and

I was not yet skilled enough in my own noes to pass the magic to them.

So, realizing I had much no work of my own, I fled my managerial/wise-older-sister role—a plain and much-needed no to the woes of young, unattached women (which I had already bumbled through myself)—and took a job as a book editor.

What do book editors do? Well, we say no a lot—to people who've been writing their dead mothers' stories for 20 years or memoirs of struggles with breast cancer. I've said no to horrific, highly personal stories of child abduction, rape, and murder—as well as to a collection of recipes of favorite family relishes and a woman who felt her life was transformed when she met Tom Cruise. (She even sent a picture.)

I have said no to movie stars (sweet!), truck drivers, bigamists, food television stars, college professors, miraculous survivors of terrifying events, scientists, world-famous athletes (usually much smaller than you imagined), stay-at-home moms, murderers, saints, politicians, and brilliant surgeons. I've said plenty of yesses, or I wouldn't have any books to publish, therefore making no money and risking the wrath of a group of people who love to say no—my corporate superiors.

But this great splatter film of no—a good definition of the life of a book editor—hadn't migrated to my private life quickly enough. I needed to figure out who and what in my immediate world needed a rejection letter right now.

Whom could I look to for advice on no? Men? Do men use

the word *no* better than women do? In my experience, the answer is yes. They are clever about it: You ask a man for something, and he looks at you blankly before walking off. And, of course, there's the dreaded "Were you saying something?" as you hear him padding away down the hall.

I have watched my husband glare an incompetent waiter into unemployment, and I have waited for two hours in a restaurant before walking to the maître d's podium and peeping, "I hate to be a nuisance, but is our table ready yet?" I have sat in countless meetings where the males not only dominated the conversation, they said, "That's not going to happen" and "Oh, you really think so?" repeatedly and with great vigor to vendors, clients, colleagues, and even their bosses. I have been car shopping with my father, who told the nattering salesman to "put a sock in it and let me look at the car" while I was nodding and mm-hmming everything he said.

But a woman? No is a concept we struggle with. We've had weird notions of good and bad laid on us all our lives. We've been programmed to please to the point of ridiculousness, and when we start deprogramming and saying no, people sigh and say, "She used to be so nice."

> *The one thing I do not want to*
> *be called is First Lady.*
> *It sounds like a saddle horse.*
> JACQUELINE KENNEDY ONASSIS

Well, it's not that I don't want to be nice. But what I really, really want more is to be a woman who is free and excited and engaged and productive and fulfilled and loved and rested and amused and respected and at peace. If I must risk the harsh words reserved only for powerful women—"What a ballbuster!" "What's the difference between her and a bowling ball? I could screw the bowling ball if I had to!" "Check her husband for a dick!"—then so be it.

For I can imagine no ending worse than lying in an ICU, probably hairless, life dripping away into rubber hoses, and thinking, *I just wish I hadn't let that silly Walter pick our vacation spot every year. . . . I so hated bone fishing* or *Why did I marry at 21?* or *I wanted to sing. But then I met Matt, and soon we started having all those kids.* The consequences of all that yessing terrifies.

If I want to live my life as I choose—if I want to own what I do, both good and bad, smart and stupid—there is no better helper than no.

So who am I to write this book? Well, I'm not a psychologist or a guru or an expert on much of anything, really. I'm just a woman who's trying and sometimes succeeding to change. I can't flash cool psychobabble words like *boundaries, personal space,* or *issues* at you with any authority. But I can attempt to become stronger, clearer, more focused, and aware.

I can use the layman's term: *no.*

No is what you think of yourself, the value you put on

your time, your abilities, your thoughts, your spirit. You are who you no.

As you continue through *The Power of No,* I hope you feel it. As you read the stories here—all true—I hope you laugh and see the ridiculousness (not to say danger) of the situations we put ourselves into because we fear hurt feelings or being perceived as a bitch. If I say no, will he stop loving me? If I tell the boss the plan is too expensive to execute, will I be fired? Will I twist myself into knots and limit myself and my life because I am afraid of one word?

No.

THE RICH WORLD OF NO

Wherever there are humans, there is the word *no.* It is a perfectly appropriate response to a great many people, places, and events. You will learn the ways to say it, from full frontal, in your face to quietly like a sigh. You will learn the effectiveness of silence as a stand-in for no and how to use inaction to thwart unwanted action. Doing absolutely nothing is sometimes the perfect no. A well-timed, cordial, negative murmur can save the face of the asker and make you seem the smoothest character on the planet.

Never, ever say yes when you mean no—and never say yes first, meaning to say no later, a common reaction to the surprise or sneaky request. In the end, whether they know it or not, the greatest gift you can give others is to tell them the truth so they can make other plans. Until you get more fluent in no, learn to buy yourself **no time,** delaying an answer until you've had a chance to think it through.

For never, ever in the history of the planet has no been more important. America did not say no to politicians who ran this country over and then got very rich. No, we didn't say no; we just went along for the ride. Some ride it's been, too. Just say the word *gasoline* or *Iraq* and feel the rage, yours and the person you are talking with.

Never, ever before has Mother Nature been so under siege. Rather than saying "No! Stop!" and meaning it, we plod along, shaking our heads and wondering who will really have to live in underground bunkers to escape the sun. Our children? Their children? Perhaps we'll be lowered into big vats of SPF 150 with zinc every time we need to go to the box and get the mail.

I won't even touch the present treatment of women right here in the good old USA. Yes, a woman made a bid for the presidency. But for every Hillary Clinton, there are millions of women who kinda like being called "my bitch" and have never given a thought to how much smaller their paychecks are than those of the guys in the neighboring cubicles.

Using no effectively requires that you know yourself. Understand that for each and every no, there is an equal and opposite no-reaction. Not necessarily a bad one, but a no-reaction nonetheless. It's true that if you say no, you might not be asked to do this particular thing by this particular person again. But someone or something else will come into your life at another moment and will feel like the right thing to yes—like a new job that pays better or a man who treats you like a human being, not a bitch or a ho.

And never, ever before in history have there been more tools for people to get at you. I actually long for junk mail now; it's so much easier to identify than prerecorded sales pitches on my cell phone. I get e-mails from people in places such as Kazakhstan and Lagos, Nigeria. They have a great money-making plan for me. I have a spam filter for them.

You must learn to understand the emotional why of your no. Is it merely an issue of time? Money? Both? Or does this no speak to the essence of who you are or who you refuse to be? Do you dislike the person asking? Is it the way you were asked? Is it the ridiculousness of the request? ("Yes! I'll send money to you in Nigeria! Just tell me how much!") Any of these reactions, great or small, are completely valid reasons to say no.

You may think, *My life is not as complex as all this.* But is it? Take one day—say, tomorrow—and pay attention to how many times you must make a decision or respond to a request. Upon examination, each day of your life is different in a million ways. Today, sure, the toughest moment is when you decline whipped cream. But on another day, you might leave your husband, dump your boyfriend, or quit your job.

*I am happy being able
to play roles with people my
age because once you do
something mature, there is no
turning back.*
LINDSAY LOHAN

In the end, learning to say no is about growing up. It's about self-knowledge and self-respect, two prized and often hard-won commodities.

This isn't kid stuff. Be prepared.

THE *POWER* OF

NO

CHAPTER I

THE YESSING SEASON

No in Love

Why are the laws of attraction so often ignored when one is trying to attract? Chasing is not attracting; it is incessant yessing. And it's annoying to most. Want something? Wait.

In this low-rise, instant-messaging world, everything and everyone is ready to wiggle, giggle, and hang at any given moment. Pants graze hips, and shirts ride rib cages; virtually anyone can be contacted in a second, no matter where they are or what they're doing; random desires can be typed and sent in an impetuous nanosecond, arriving with a beep to the object of desire.

With all of this in-your-face-here-you-go-I'm-on-my-way yessing, never before has there been so much for the taking and giving and never have so many been unhappy once taken or gotten. Quite frankly, it is easier today to have sex than an interesting or meaningful conversation. Whatever you want is available, and yet nothing seems to last because the next bootylicious message alert is on its way. And you, my friend, are history.

Why?

Because you should have said no when you said yes.

You fell for the notion that because you said yes, someone would like you and like you for a long time. You said yes because you wanted that shiny thing, and you said yes because you thought it was the way to lasting love, enduring friendship, and acceptance—a happy life all around. You looked around at a culture gone mad with yes and forgot one of the most profound and enduring truths about human nature:

People want what they cannot have.

You will learn that getting what you want often depends on your willingness to go without it—your gamble that a short burst of initial rejection will get you your much-longed-for sustained embrace. Did June Carter just run off immediately with that pill-popping, liquor-guzzling Johnny Cash?

It's the ancient adage, made icky by Sting in a song: Free, free, set it free. Then let it come to you.

Chase nothing. Pursue no one. Stand fast and let it come to you.

You must, through word or deed, say no to get the yes you crave.

NO AND THE FIRST MEETING

Never is the razor's edge between no and yes as keen as during the first meeting between people with a potential for romance. What you do or, more important, what you don't do will have lasting repercussions.

There are countless ways to encounter the opposite sex and precious few ways to select and retain one of worth. You must learn to remain just out of reach while you access the other. You must say no while inside you're screaming *yes!*

At this moment, much rides on your ability to stand your ground and remain cool and calm. This is where your deft use of the word *no,* in all its many forms, will set the tenor of this relationship, should it get that far.

If you want to be valued, what is he going to think if you say yes to a date an hour after he calls? Why should he call you on Tuesday for Saturday night? If you let him swing by and hang out, why should he take you to dinner and a movie? (For goodness sake, the definition of marriage is "hanging out." Why would you do it at the beginning of, hopefully, a love affair?)

NO ATTRACTION

Why a person does or does not feel an attraction to another person is a mystery as old and deep as how they make Cheetos.

In those first few moments of meeting a "person of interest," time collapses. Your imagination flies far into the future and has you shooing your future husband and five kids down the front walk of your split-level ranch house. Or your mind skips forward to an hour later (ah, make that at least two hours later), and you experience a vision of yourself, unclothed and just worshipped, searching for your underpants among hastily made piles of clothing.

Whatever your initial fantasy—a hot game of burglar and the housewife or the dawn of a domestic dynasty—you must summon forth your strongest sense of no; this guy might be Ted Bundy's younger brother. Or he might be a cross between Denzel Washington and Bishop Tutu. The point is, you don't know who he is, and until you know, say no.

Exchange the phone numbers and e-mail addresses. Talk about all the things you have in common, and if and when that call or e-mail arrives, pace yourself. Let the message sit for a day or two; after all, you are very busy. Many jostle for some of your time. What happens as the message sits? Do more follow with ever-increasing need? Or does he silently say, *The ball is in your court, lady. Make a move.* Observe him from a distance, then at arm's length. This is what our boys in camouflage call recon and our mothers called not being a little fool. Really, this is a moment at which hyperawareness and self-containment must rule. This little bit of no will save you a lot of money on therapists, meds, and divorce lawyers.

GETTING TO NO YOU

Bud is a young man of 28 with a great Wall Street job and a beautiful, buff body. One night, he meets Catherine at a bar. Mutual friends introduce them. They stand against the back wall, just out of the strongest light, and talk intensely for hours.

The next day, Bud leaves a message on Catherine's cell phone. Then another. She has left town and will return that night. She listens to his messages—all five of them—and plans to call him the next day after she's had a good night's sleep.

Bud is nervous. This 24-hour silence has freaked him out, and his insecurities are squirming just under his skin. *She doesn't like me. She doesn't think I'm hot.* In a complex spasm of anxiety, he calls her cell phone at 2:00 a.m. She picks up, thinking of loved ones thrown into a highway ditch through a breach in twisted metal licked by flames. In his race toward immediate acceptance and gratification, Bud hasn't thought of this—the chick picking up a cell phone in the middle of the night. But Catherine is a seasoned veteran of dating, and she is amused by the call yet mindful. She hasn't been on a date in a while and is willing to proceed.

The date goes down. Bud is wired, talking nonstop throughout dinner. He blurts out his life story and paints his career as if he were Warren Buffett. Sometimes he veers so out of control, he refers to himself in the third person. "Little Bud graduated with honors," he tells her. Catherine's homeland security monitor is bright red. She is nodding her head, smiling, and saying yes as her gates are slamming shut and all emotion is heading for the nuclear-safe facility deep under the Rocky Mountains.

The walk home is uneventful. But this is New York City, and Bud insists on walking Catherine upstairs to her apartment. At the door, he asks to have a beer before ending the evening. Catherine has determined he's harmless; she never imagined that Little Bud has brought along a friend, Big Billy.

She settles on the couch, and Bud realizes he has a private captive audience. There are no other people to stand between Catherine and his unbearable hotness. He begins a soliloquy about how much he works out, creating a swooning manliness that cannot be ignored. He playfully takes off his shirt, exposing cut arms and six-pack abs.

He walks in a tight circle, clenching and unclenching his butt, carefully explaining to Catherine the difference between "buns of steel" and "soft like cotton." The five-minute warning bell rings in Catherine's head. And then the truly terrible happens.

Little Bud pulls out his manhood and says, "This is Big Billy, and he wants to say hi."

That's right, Bud has a talking penis.

"Touch me and watch me grow!" Big Billy crows at her.

But what really rises is Catherine as she picks up Bud's shirt and twirls him toward the door. So caught up in his own show, Bud barely protests.

Several days later—after he has called and texted her several times daily—Catherine sends him a short e-mail saying goodbye. Bud is upset and continues to believe that Catherine is lame. He even removes her from his "friends" list on Facebook.

NO QUESTION

While obvious to both you and me, introducing Big Billy to Catherine on the first date was a really bad idea. But this potential romance died long before that haunting moment. Catherine did not race to yes, and it was in this pause that Little Bud truly lost his mind. He was yelling yes way too loud and long and fast and became undesirable because of his extreme availability. Catherine surely had a clue that he was needy, but could she have anticipated a talking penis?

Perhaps. But it was certainly clear from the beginning that Bud was massively insecure and needed more attention than even a room full of mothers could give. Catherine's instincts and experience told her he was problematic, but she had decided to give him a chance.

Before you say yes to that first date, ask yourself:

* Did he wait less than 48 hours to call? (And yes, there is immediate true love that knows no time or rules, but it's about as common as someone who understands how Cheetos are made.)

* After his first call, did he repeatedly leave messages during the next 24 hours? Did his tone change from normal to pleading to hostile as the messages piled up? Really, a call or two is enough. Anything more bespeaks of ridiculously shaky self-esteem.

* Can he talk about himself nonstop for 10 minutes? Twenty? An hour? Does he interrupt his monologue to ask you about yourself? How often, if ever?

* Does he talk about himself nonstop both on the phone and in person, no matter what is going on around him and who is present?

If the answer to even one of the above questions is yes, friend, **warm up your no.**

NO MAN'S LAND

The period between meeting a potential mate for the first time and the first moment of willing contact (i.e., a date) is unstable ground. You have given your number, and you might even have his. But the number has not popped up yet, and you are living moment to moment. Your cell phone has become a talisman, a charmed object that can deliver great pleasure or pain. You carry it around like it's a pacemaker; your heart will stop beating if the phone isn't on your body at all times.

You call this living?

First of all, by so desperately wanting this human to call, you've given away your power to someone you don't know; your happiness or lack thereof rides on the action or inaction of someone who just might be a boob. Second, whether it takes a week or two or never for this person to call you, this is your life, the days allotted for you to walk this earth. Third, people clutching and endlessly checking cell phones look nervous, needy, and pathetic, three very unsexy adjectives.

Now this is precious time that you could spend with friends (rather than boring them to death with anxious, obsessive dating blather), running, skiing, working, shopping, meeting new people, traveling, or inventing a vaccine that will eradicate bird flu.

The world needs you present. And if that phone does ring and the number does pop up, don't you dare answer that call. Don't blurt yes in a moment that you need to stretch into the no implied by making him wait. Let him spend some time in No Man's Land. When you do return that call, he'll stumble outta there like a man adrift in a desert, thirsty and hungry for you.

9

> *One is not born, but rather*
> *becomes, a woman.*
> SIMONE DE BEAUVOIR

Not only does obsessing about "the call" stop you in your tracks, it freezes your mind with one pointless thought: *Will my phone ring?*

And what does that call really mean?

Let's check with Ron, an experienced chick magnet in his prime. He's been with a lot of women and thought about the dance a lot, analyzing the push-me-pull-you nature of every encounter. He's got rules and strategies for aggressive women, shy women, plain women, and babes. At first, he holds himself back and lets the woman tell him who she is. He makes sure he holds the high ground for as long as possible. Based on what he sees and hears, he moves. Or not.

"Whenever I exchange phone numbers, I have that little moment of regret," Ron says. "I mean, they are just numbers and, man, in some reality, some women confuse them with something else. I gave my number to a woman I worked with. We agreed it would be great if we could go out for drinks sometime. Not long after I left work, she called me seven times in a row when I didn't pick up. I couldn't believe that number kept popping up. She didn't know who I was. She didn't know me at all. When I finally picked up in hopes of getting her to stop, she began to question where I was and why I wasn't answering. In her head, that one went right from swapping phone numbers to 10 years of marriage, bad marriage at that.

"This was all about ego. She thought I was saying no to her, rejecting her because I did not respond at the moment. It was good information, and I used it by never taking her out for drinks."

NO CELL PHONES, PLEASE

The last invention to have as much impact on romance as the cell phone was the birth control pill. The cell phone is that powerful. The cell phone is that scary.

Ron, the chick magnet, wields his like a .38. He knows what's incoming and exactly how many rounds to fire off. The thing sits in his lap or on the table in front of him. He monitors who's looking for him, who's telling him yes. Ron has learned that the cell phone is one big yes monitor, quivering with possibility; and if a woman abuses it, he writes her off as too easy, uninterestingly fast.

If and when he returns a call, he can tell if the woman is talking on the phone or has turned it off. If the phone is on and she doesn't pick up, he infers that she's doing what he does: watching the number pop up and making a judgment call.

"I use the cell phone to read people," Ron says, "and a call too quickly made or answered is a yes that hints of a lack of confidence or experience or both."

This technology was designed for convenience. It's also rigged with caller ID, options to go straight to voice mail, and the ability to block numbers. In short, the cell phone allows you to be very available, yet it's also interested in your privacy and wants you to be in control.

Thus, every one of your fevered dials is registered on the guy's unit forever. Okay, not forever. But a day or two of messages, however random, is all it takes for him to understand that you don't just want to date him, you want to move into his underwear drawer or take over his frontal cortex.

Be cool. Not dialing is a potent form of self-respect, even if your lizard brain is screaming, *Me want him! Me want him!*

Not dialing is a vote of confidence in yourself and a nice little space—remember No Man's Land?—where he can do some thinking. Yeah, your eyes really are that blue. Yeah, you told him the story about the business dinner in a four-star restaurant: Your pompous boss was there. A man walked up to your table with a wine list. He announced that he was your sommelier, and your boss said, "So, you're from Venice."

Yeah, you are that funny. You are a woman worth getting to know. Let him call. Let it go to voice mail. Wait a day or two. Use the cell phone to create a space where you seem to be saying no to him. Cell phone management is not a game; it's a life strategy and another way you build no into your life.

You Bought the Thing and Signed the Contract. Now Make It Work for You

1. If you exchange phone numbers, do nothing. His response time—or lack of—is key information.

2. Never answer the first call. Let it go to voice mail. Wait.

3. If you find yourself staring at the phone and thinking about how he will look in tails, turn it off. Put it away in a drawer. Leave it there until your madness passes.

4. I turn my phone off a lot. *A lot.* Some people won't leave a message on a turned-off phone for reasons that completely escape me. But if there's a bunch of missed calls and no message, it's creepy. Is this an Amish thing? Take my picture (or record my voice) and you steal a bit of my soul? Really, leave a damn message, and I'll call back.

5. Never, ever do the *67 trick. (By punching the star, six, and seven keys, you can call his cell as an unidentified number.) It is the equivalent of driving past his house to see if he's home. Just as kissing leads to sex and marijuana to hard drugs, *67 is the first stop before the drive-by that can lead to obsessive dialing and hanging up and showing your friends his graduation pictures on flickr.com. Just don't do it. (Besides, as I discovered, you'll eventually get caught. If you're like me, you'll then burst into tears. This is not sexy.) Never answer an unidentified caller on your cell phone. There is no one worth talking to that

13

will not identify themselves. This bespeaks of a sneaky nature and arrested development, two characteristics that deserve a **full-frontal no.**

6. If and when you meet again, watch how he uses his cell phone. Does he put it away, like anyone with any basic manners? Or is he incessantly checking it, grimacing or smiling at the caller ID? Does he excuse himself for a chat with his "brother"? So bad is the behavior of some male cell phone users that I had one call me dude throughout the conversation to throw his girlfriend off as he took my call. I still sometimes wonder if she is sitting there patiently as he honks into the phone at "his bro."

HANG NO

History is full of heart-stopping tales of love, from the knight who jousts a dark, foul opponent for the affection of a maiden to a prince who will not be king if it means giving up his woman.

Consider the danger—the risk to body, mind, and soul—these lovers endured for the sake of their beloved. Consider the words they used to describe the other: *my heart, my soul, my life.*

At no time did Lancelot send a messenger to Guinevere

asking her to come to his hamlet and hang out. Nor would you find Scarlett and Rhett lolling in the parking lot of Atlanta's Spicy Wing Wonderland, licking their fingers and watching cars go by.

Love had words and deeds that meant something, had teeth, bespoke of unwavering commitment that defined the very essence of the lover.

Consider: "I will wait until the end of time." "When I am with you, there is no other world." "How do I love thee? Let me count the ways." "I will love thee with my last breath."

No "wanna hang out" here. No nebulous, noncommittal, cowardly, muddled, emotion-masking avoidance technique in the pages of history's great loves. Nor should there be any in your life.

If you get to the first real telephonic exchange and he asks you to hang out, if you say yes, you are asking to take the walk with the wieners. If someone wants you to hang out, say, "I don't hang out. But I do go to dinner and the movies." If someone is asking you out, he should have a plan, a plan that will be revealed to you and please you. You don't sit on couches watching *Extreme Fight Night*. You don't consider watching someone try on jackets at the Gap a date.

Dating doesn't take a lot of money. It takes the gonads to say, "I like this person. I want us to spend time together that feels special." It takes imagination and courage. For goodness sake, if someone doesn't have the guts to ask you out, how do you think the love affair is going to go?

AND WHAT DO YOU THINK MARRIAGE IS, ANYWAY?

Marriage is hanging out. Marriage is "You want to split a six-pack, order pizza, and watch the game?" Marriage is "Let's walk the dog to the corner and see the construction on that new house." Marriage is "Come talk to me while I put a new coat of stain on the back deck." Why in the world would you ever settle for the hanging out that is marriage when you could be dancing, getting hammered on appletinis, and having unusual sex?

17

DATING

So you have made it through No Man's Land and are on a date. The romantic rubber is hitting the road, and there doesn't appear to be any immediate potholes. Be ever wary. For the first few dates, everyone is on their very best behavior. But a man in front of a new woman often behaves like a sausage in a casing under heat: As he swells with mannish feelings, small splits in the exterior often reveal interesting things cooking underneath. If you don't like what you see, it's a lot easier to say no now than two years into the marriage.

THE POWER OF NO

NEVER LET THE NO GUARD DOWN

So you're dating the guy. Maybe you feel you are really in a groove. It's fun, it's comfortable, and it feels like it's going places. What could possibly go wrong?

Enter **the naked brother**.

Elizabeth was happily dating a fine young man who seemed to have figured things out. He had a great job and was funny, kind, athletic, and handsome. To top it all off, he didn't have a critical bone in his body. Whatever Elizabeth did or wanted was just fine with him.

On New Year's Eve, the two went out and got drunk, lit, faded, wasted, trashed. They stumbled home and, in full New Year's Eve dress, her in high heels and all, collapsed on his bed. How much time passed, Elizabeth will never know. But she awoke in a pitch-black room with just a sliver of light falling through the cracked bedroom door. Before her eyes adjusted to the surroundings, she heard a thud and then felt rustling on the bed. Whatever it was, it was big. And it was headed right for her. She hit the lights and there it was, crouched in the middle of the bed: a butt-nekked, visiting-for-the-weekend brother who just wanted to "join the fun."

Elizabeth's boyfriend did not awaken during her resulting flight through the living room and out into the street. He was to hear the whole story sometime around noon the next day from the naked brother. In his kind, uncritical way, he deemed the entire event no big deal. He is still, no doubt, wondering what ever happened to Elizabeth.

THE BEGINNING OF THE END

As dating progresses, be busy some nights: Say, "Thank you, but I've made plans, sorry, no." Establish your independence from the get-go.

How does he react to your not being available to him at all times? What happens in the space between dates—called the **no-date space** by the experienced? Does he call? How often? A man hanging around on your phone is a possible indicator of neediness or perhaps lack of trust. Does he not call? Is he pouting? Pulling a **reverse no-date space** on you? It's all important information about whether or not this man will or will not receive the **ultimate date no.**

The ultimate date no is as it seems. Obviously, if the two of you are humming as you paddle your canoe of love, you are in no need of this advice.

But if, after a certain period of dating, your internal clock announces—even if you don't hear it the first, second, or fifth time—that this guy has got to go, then he has to go. Sometimes it's a lack of punctuality mingled with never asking if you, too, would like a delicious beverage like the one he is sipping. Sometimes it's your sense that he's taken an IQ test but failed to register a score. Sometimes it's his shoes. A lot of times it's his shoes.

One time, in an extreme example of the **no gone terribly wrong,** or **insane no,** the woman had to leave the man because he would not let her touch his penis. That's right, he lay there clutching it as if it was his favorite blankey. A rare event, penis clutching is pretty much a deal breaker. As she said later, "How could I ever learn to master his domain?"

BUT BOY, COULD HE . . .

Sometimes you encounter a master of the horizontal arts so skilled that no matter how unsatisfying a human you find him, you want him to hang around. For a while, at least. Do not confuse this **no purgatory** for anything other than it is: sex. There are women who endure dating agony—one friend sat for hours watching a man play with his Xbox, while still another sat looking at several hundred photos of the deer a man shot—just to have a little time with his big unit or writhe with pleasure at the touch of his artist's hands.

Do not be mistaken: No amount of great sex can compensate for the fact that the guy is in all other respects a moron. See him for sex, pay attention to his technique (after all, you can teach it to your perfect new boyfriend), and don't try to make contact with his mind. That will frustrate you and make you unclear as to why you still have his number in your phone: sex.

> *Usually I'm on top to keep the*
> *guy from escaping.*
> LISA LAMPANELLI

SHORT BUT MAYBE SWEET?

Speaking of sex, there is no more powerful aphrodisiac than the word *no*. It never fails. Saying no to a man who wants to make love to you will often unleash a display of testosterone-driven exhibitionism rarely seen beyond certain high branches in the rain forest. Your no is the gasoline in his fire, the grease on his crankshaft.

Often, he will mount a full-scale invasion along the lines of Operation Shock and Awe. Do not be fooled: These maneuvers are about him, not you. You have questioned his hotness, and he must launch a counteroffensive and regain his high ground (the high ground being you, without clothes). If you relent, remember the spoils of war are brief: You'll no doubt get some good sex (maybe even great—he does after all, have to show you how misguided you were in doubting his prowess). Once he feels his mojo has returned, say good-bye to your small victory.

EVEN THEY NO IT

A young man named KK was regaling his friends with tall tales of his gigantic penis. Apparently, its magic was so strong that women often go about the next day babbling about it to any friend who will listen. He referred to this phenomenon as advertising. Then he smiled—quite bashfully for a man with such an enormous unit—and said, "And you know what really, really, *really* works? Sometimes I tell them no."

LEAVING A LOVER IS A SPECIAL KINDA NO

Odds are, the dude you are seeing now is not the one. He's never the one until you look up 15 years later and he's still hanging around. You think, *Him again. He was the one?!?*

Some women keep men around they don't really like, a form of romantic gum chewing. You expend the same amount of energy every day, it stays pretty soft, and the flavor is gone. For a **person of no,** this kind of sexual stall is unthinkable. Not to mention pointless, pathetic, and downright peculiar.

Even a person who has trouble with no sometimes gets the opportunity to plan a good leaving. Most often, it is a reaction to behavior so grotesque your cerebral cortex will never truly process it, but, alas, it will play, like *The World's Worst Animal Attacks,* over and over in your mind's eye.

Leaving a lover or spouse is a special kind of no and deserves deep thought. And, in keeping with all civilized societies, the tenor of the leaving—the punishment, if you will—must be in keeping with the nature and severity of the crime (usually crimes).

> *Men don't want responsibility,*
> *and neither do I.*
> JULIE CHRISTIE

Was he a disconnected, couch-lolling, grunting, kinda wishy-washy, lazy dude? Expend energy equal to his: Shrug your shoulders and say, "You're boring. Get out." Remove whatever preferred object he nestled his big butt in. Get it out of your sight, and replace it with something like a great patterned couch. A larger entertainment center comes to mind. With no ESPN2 on the cable, of course.

Or maybe he's the needy child in men's clothing who constantly behaves as if you are his mommy and he's about to jump off the diving board. My usual approach to jettisoning this particular type is easy. Talk about yourself a lot. Bust into his long, boring story about how the paralegal thought he did something really smart and that she looks up to him with a thrill-tingling tale of your own. Sometimes I talk about my childhood, sometimes about shopping. Camp memories are appropriate subject matter. He will grow so tired of not being able to talk about himself that he'll lose interest in you and wander off to blather at the paralegal.

Is he an "I'm really busy" kinda guy? No need to waste another second: A text message is the perfect vehicle to send your bad news. Is he a decent sort whose only crimes are his sour breath, long stories with no punch lines, and overly large, Velcroed-together sport sandals? (Call them whatever you want, but they're still sandals. Have you ever heard a man cry, "Where are my sandals?" Your blood will freeze and have trouble flowing the rest of your life.) Give him a cheerful phone call and **land your no** as softly as possible.

Got you a cheater who never seems to learn? This is so easy: Start dating. Meet Jim for drinks after work. (He doesn't need to know Jim weighs 320 and works in accounts payable.) Have long, giggly phone calls that abruptly quiet when he walks in the room. If he's stupid enough to bring it up, then it's time for you to say, "We need to talk about the affair you're having." Hit him hard and relentlessly with the truth. Pull him into the light over and over, and if for some reason you decide you will live with this, do get a boyfriend because you're going to be lonely.

I see you now, looking up and thinking, *Is she really saying what I think she's saying?* Yes. I am. This is the 21st century. Men and women share the same rights and the same opportunities to screw up. You might as well get a new lover out of the deal. Part of the power of no is that you are not a victim. Ever. Or at least not after the 24 hours it takes you to grab the truth, shake it in your mighty jaws, and fling it at him.

A HEEL AND A HEEL

Suzanne's first boyfriend really did not think she would notice the girl sitting on his lap at a party. Drunk and stupid, he and his newly found soul mate wandered past Suzanne holding hands as he walked his new love to her car. Though young and inexperienced, Suzanne understood instinctively that such a violation of the dating fundamentals could not go unpunished. She outflanked her sloppy lover and placed herself between him and the new girl's car door. She then pushed him down in the mud and, needing a weapon, pulled off her wedge-heeled pump. She whacked him repeatedly in the head, at which point the other woman stepped over them both, got in the car, and drove off. Drunk, dirty, and sporting a wedge-print on his face, Suzanne's first boyfriend understood he would not be her last.

LUNCH NO

One of my most amusing and cherished memories is of a break-up lunch in my late twenties. It was a fairly hot few months with this guy, and I wasn't expecting to get dumped. But as he actually said the words "Beth, we are growing in different directions," the carrot stick he had just dipped into ranch dressing was in his mouth, backward, the coated end moving like a windshield wiper across his face, leaving great long smears of white goo on his cheek. He was so **deep in his noness** that he wasn't aware of the abstract expressionism happening there on his face. To this day, every time I drive in the rain, I think of that fool and smile.

LUNCH ABSOLUTELY NOT

My friend Victoria has a different memory of a midday breakup meal. After knowing and working with this man for years, he calls and asks for a date. And another. And another. They have dinner. They go to a party. They see movies on the first night of release. Plans are made; e-mails soaked in joy and longing are exchanged. Victoria, not quite believing her good fortune, feels nothing out of the ordinary when she accepts his invitation to lunch.

After the food is ordered, he begins. He has some "issues" he needs to lay on the table. He is too stressed, too busy for love. She is wonderful, yet . . . He is a writer—an artist, really—and Victoria stands between him and his work. "I can't give you what you need! What you deserve!" he opines in the busy restaurant. Victoria feels that, at the very least, she has stumbled into the middle of a Kabuki theater act staged to entertain downtown workers at noontime. How long has this guy been practicing his part? Did he do it in front of the bathroom mirror?

Victoria took the only form of action appropriate: the **absolutely not.** She stood up; said, "I don't have to listen to this crap"; threw money on the table for her half of lunch; and walked out. To this day, she still doesn't see how that guy built up such an oration for a woman he had dated for a week.

He was e-mailing her again days later, asking her out for lunch. Confused and annoyed, she declined, as she continues to do every time she hears from him.

YOU ARE NOT IN A MOVIE

Deliver a punishment that fits the crime. Blubbery, issue-laden lunches are for people who have had a long and special journey to this, the **no fork in the road.** Don't make a jackass of yourself while delivering the no-date news. After all, it's no fun when someone sniggers while walking away, completely disgusted at your dramatics.

Here are a few ways to deliver your message.

1. Text him. Possible messages: "I know you're busy, so don't call me again." Or wait several days before communicating. Send a text taking the line of a much-celebrated country song: "Remember when your phone didn't ring yesterday? Well, that

was me." Believe me, this will make him really mad, but oh, is it worth it.

2. E-mail him. It's not like writing in your diary, either. Don't sneeze up all the flickers of emotion you've ever felt for him. Tell him, "Thanks, it was fun, but it's enough fun. Let's not have any more fun so this fun we had feels really fun whenever I think about having fun."

3. Cut the wires. This is a powerful form of no that should be called upon only in situations where your no is not heard, understood, or accepted. You don't answer the phone when you see his number; you do not dial it back. Change his caller ID name to Absolutely Not or Bluck or Cold Day in Hell on your contact list. This will both instruct and amuse when he calls. You may get the *67 trick here. Do not be fooled. He's gonna call and call, but sometimes the only no is the **fortress no.**

Circle the wagons and fill the moat. Put your guards on the ramparts. Drop his name in your spam filter. You may feel besieged for a while, but when the no finally takes, it will hold.

4. Drop the best $25 you will ever spend. There is a point in some breakups where you realize he is just too dumb and way too narcissistic to believe that you've really left him. You cannot stand the sound of his voice in your cell phone any longer. It is your cell phone and it is carried on your person, a rather intimate

location. Call your carrier and change your number. Send a text message to everyone but him with your new coordinates. The recording "That number is no longer in service" is a powerful message indeed.

5. Resist Kabuki theater. Oh, no, don't you do it. Don't pick a public place (and that includes a Starbucks!) and ruin someone's meal *and* opinion of you forever. To take such a private moment into a public place screams bad judgment—or worse, that you need to perform in front of strangers. So join the circus or become a pole dancer.

6. Call it. Many forget that Alexander Graham Bell invented the telephone so couples could break up without having to look at each other. In today's text-laden world, a phone call is a magnificent thing. Intention can be relayed not only with words but tone of voice. Was there a cataclysmic event that caused the breakup? Well, you can be damn angry about it on the phone. Need to explain how you have grown apart? (Growing apart is translated into most of the world's languages as "you bore me.") The phone allows you to give examples that are most often not refuted on the spot. The phone is the most effective **no-date tool** there is. You have the intimate quality of the human voice to communicate fused with, hopefully, miles and miles of distance between you and your caller.

There are so many ways to say no without having to look into the whites of his eyes and smell his **no sweat.** Why stoop to beating him with your favorite wedge and ruin a good shoe? Save your energy, and make an exit that gets your message delivered in a satisfying, effective way and keeps you as safe as possible.

BOLTING

This **plutonium of no** deserves its own close look. Now, there isn't a mental health care professional on the planet that will advocate bolting as anything but a cowardly—and futile—attempt to outrun your problems. Rightly so. But I also believe (and probably some scientist somewhere agrees) that the body—and mind—cannot heal if it is actively in pain all the damn time. Get away from the high-pitched squeal of the person/problem that is driving you mad. *Bolt.* Then get calm and begin to face your demons. But first, *bolt.*

> *Men and women, women and*
> *men. It will never work.*
> ERICA JONG

While bolting (running, going to ground, disappearing, fleeing before invaders, skedaddling, crawling into your hidey-hole, changing hemispheres, etc.) is most often a part of dating, it can be of great use in a bad marriage. A moment comes when there are no words. There is only action. Decisive—some say cold and calculating—action that gets you the hell out of there. And, if all else has failed, you should save your own life. Seems the only prudent thing to do.

You have just two ways to bolt: explain and go or just go.

I like "just go" and have used it with great success more than once. Believe me, if you are at the **bolt point** and he or she doesn't know why, no explaining is going to make it right. Just go.

I had one interesting moment when as I drove from the house, furniture and clothes crammed to the car roof, I passed my boltee and just gave him a little wave that said, "Off to CVS. Back in a jiff with your toothpaste!" Again, I relied on his self-absorption to not notice the packed car. He did not disappoint.

Figure out what you need to do to leave, arrange it quietly, and do so. You will be fine. You will rebuild whatever parts of your life need rebuilding. Your family and friends and no doubt the criminal laws of your county, state, or country will help you.

The "explain" part of "explain and go" always feels like something the departee, not the one being left, needs to do. You can't bolt and be remembered as a good guy or gal. The person you flee will always, no matter how he or she acts four years later in the cereal aisle of the grocery store, on some level deeply, deeply resent you. Live with it. This is not *Miss Congeniality;* this is your life.

When all negotiations fail, be the one to walk out of the room. Hang up first. Pack the car and drive.

USING NO TO GET TO YES, YES, YES

When the time arrives to mull the long term, you have a lot of thinking to do. If you think that you can spend what is the equivalent of eternity—the span of the rest of your life—with this man, then do it, baby, headfirst! No state of being is a better spawning ground for the word *no* than marriage. For the rest of your life, you will scream an internal *no!* at least three times a day: when you awake in the morning and find he's still there; when you find his hair on the ceiling of the shower; and, when, not if, he extols your qualities in relation to his mother: "You're like my mother, only I like you better."

If you really want this, though, and he is dithering, no can be of tremendous use in getting to the altar. Just think of it as playing a frisky game of chicken, where you won't lose your life, but certainly your heart could get bent and twisted. No and the engagement isn't for sissies, but aren't you reading this book so no one will mistake you for one?

I knew a woman in Texas who tired of her East Coast boyfriend's aversion to the special question. After a few years of anxiety and self-doubt, she went on a serious job interview in the opposite direction: San Francisco, to be exact. A great opportunity, this gig would put a continent between her and her tongue-tied problem. While he never could understand her "why can't we get married?" he did understand not having a penis that could reach 3,000 miles. (He said later he could have handled St. Louis.)

Today they are happily married, and she noes him half to death each day, just like his mother did, but now he likes it better. Of course, the price of this strategy failing is high—the end of a union that presumably you kinda like. For if your "I'm getting on with my life" maneuver backfires (he offers to pack the U-Haul), you'll lose a boyfriend *and* a husband. What a waste—you've been sitting on the couch with him for four years watching rental DVDs like *Saw III* and *The Hills Have Eyes II*—but if he hasn't gotten a grip on your goodness by now, he simply isn't husband-ready material.

Here are a few ways to imply the **ultimate no** while looking for the ultimate yes.

1. Go on job interviews in other cities. Studies have proven time and time again that the average man will drive half a day to "get it" but rarely any farther.

2. Tell him what you want—namely, to get married—then don't take his calls for a week or two. Men (as well as just about every other mammal) hate to be ignored, and your indifference will make him turn red, swell in his pants, and capitulate. Or not. At least you'll begin a serious conversation.

3. Threaten couples counseling to explore his lack of commitment. The look on his face alone will make all repercussions moot. Who cares if he marries you—you saw all the blood flow out of his face as his eyes fluttered spasmodically. Sweet.

4. Say no to Sundays on the couch and take up a fabulous sport full of buff males. Talk about them some. Glow as you do it.

5. Break up with him. Yeah, you read that right. Why would you want to be with a man who doesn't want to marry you? Break. Up. With. Him. You've given him his shot. Have the courage and belief that there is a long-lasting love for you (which of course there is), and go find it.

CHAPTER 2

I DON'T

No in Marriage

So you've gone and done it. You survived No Man's Land, kept your cool, and managed to avoid the naked brother. Lucky you. Now begins the true no triathlon, the grueling phase where you must learn to shape your life with another. And if you learn and like to say no, it's way fun.

Take me now, baby, here as I am.
PATTI SMITH

Marriage is no's rich playground, the South of France for negative utterances. Say no every day. A well-noed husband is a happy husband; his role is clear. (For a deeper exploration of legal coupling, see my previous book, *You Again: A Guide to Marriage.*)

A FEW OF THE MUST-HAVE NOES
OF MARRIAGE

There are many ways to use no in a marriage. Let's explore the most effective.

1. The preemptive no strike: Borrow a strategy from George W. Bush's foreign policy. If you even imagine that your husband is building the marital equivalent of weapons of mass destruction—golfing on your birthday, excessive mother-calling (that's more than once a week), or boots on the ground in your formal living room—well, if you've got 'em, launch 'em: big, full-frontal, in-his-face noes that leave no room for question, negotiation, or touching and healing. The preemptive no strike must be executed as soon as you catch a few words from a phone call, see his golf clubs leaning against a car, or observe him staring blankly at your white rug. Get between him and the marital WMD, align your face with his, and fire one round of no! directly at his nose, the central headquarters of his face. If he shows any confusion—perhaps he is looking around to see who you are shouting at—personalize the next round of fire with No! Bob! No! Fall back and enjoy the show as his frontal cortex comes alive with stimulus and feeling.

2. The MMMmmmmmmm no: A versatile negation, the *MMMmmmmmm* no can be used playfully, mockingly, and to

frighten, depending on the intonation of *MMMmmmmmm*. For instance, you are cuddling with your husband on a slow Sunday morning when he implores, "I know you get tired of being the burglar, but please let's play burglar and the housewife." You'll want to match your *MMMmmmmmm* to the moment by purring it out, thus saving the mood and putting the kibosh on having to go outside and break in through the bedroom window. If he begins to fantasize about getting a too big couch to fit by halving it with a chain saw, your *MMMmmmmmm* should be like the razor's edge; the no, a bomb detonation. It helps to force the *MMMmmmmmm* through clenched teeth, and you should feel a strain in the neck muscles.

3. "Maybe later": The genius of this phrase is that it is not actually a negative and all men have deficit attention disorder, thus releasing you from ever hearing the request framed exactly the same way again.

> ***Him:*** Will you get on the ladder and hold up the new gutter covers so I can see if they fit?

> ***You:*** Maybe later, dear. I have a wash going.

Oh, don't be fooled: Whatever he wanted will pop back into his head as a fully formed new thought, and he will ask you with fresh enthusiasm for whatever it is. You just unsheathe your "maybe later" and let the whole process begin anew.

4. "On the way back": Again, this is a phrase (see "maybe later," page 39) in which the genius resides in the fact that it is not negative. My husband is the master of "on the way back."

"Can we stop at the roadside jam store and cider distillery?"

"On the way back."

"Can I see if those silvery shoes are still at Neiman Marcus?

"On the way back."

So, use my husband's brilliant field tactic. When your man, in his little man voice, asks to stop at J.J.'s Useless but Necessary and Expensive Personal Electronics for Men on your way to the plant store to buy roses for the side of the house, a "sure, on the way back, honey" will keep everyone happy. If the excitement of the rest of the journey doesn't distract him—surely he'll fall for a spade that lights up so he can dig in the dark or an automatic shrub-watering system that uses an intricate grid of buried hoses with shiny self-timers—coming home another way will.

5. The elusive no: You can say no without ever opening your mouth. Simply go wherever he is not. Let his calls pile up on

the cell phone; let his "Honey! Honey! Where's the mayo?" go unanswered. At first, he'll think, *Oh, she's not around. I can do all the things I want to do. I can sleep here on the couch in my underpants, man boobs dusted with Doritos crumbs. I can watch the 1986 Mets–Red Sox game seven over and over again.*

But wait! It grows dark outside! I know where nothing is except the clicker! I must have help sustaining life!

And then your phone starts to ring. . . .

Remember, if they can't find you, they can't fool with you.

6. The absolutely not: Deliver this with extreme prejudice. Leave him alone where he sits. Then, like a small child in a dark forest, he will begin to feel lonely and cold. He'll start to mutter your name and have an internal discussion about whether or not he should actually rise from the chair and go look for you. Then, depending on his fear of living in a world in which he has to get everything himself, he'll begin the search. You will let him find you when you are good and ready and, once found, will say, "I am absolutely not going in there unless you put away your remote-controlled fart machine."

> *I think that gay marriage is
> something that should be
> between a man and a woman.*
> ARNOLD SCHWARZENEGGER

Failing to discern an absolutely not from an *MMMmmmmmm* no can have painful, expensive consequences. It happened to a woman identified only as Stephanie. Stephanie's husband is a college professor and a deeply unhandy man. He can explain the rise of Marxism in post–World War II Europe but has never drilled a hole or hammered a nail in his life. For a reason known only to the mossiest, most remote corners of his subconscious, he decided to fix a warping floor in a storage attic—against Stephanie's better judgment. Up the ladder he went into the stale, dead-fly space above the bedrooms. He walked heavily across the attic several times before there was a short silence followed by the sound of wood breaking and something certainly not human squealing with fear. Stephanie ran into the guest room just in time to see her husband's little legs scissoring through the bedroom ceiling. The cost of repairing him was just slightly more than the bill for the attic floor.

All marriages are different noes of varying sound levels. Emotion may or may not play a part of the no delivery. Explore your **no options** carefully. Test out as many as you can. After all, you've got the rest of your life to tell this guy no each and every day.

> *I married beneath me.*
> *All women do.*
> NANCY ASTOR

Universal No Themes in Marriage

❋ Anything that involves the words *au, pair,* and *girl*

❋ Buying furniture and home accessories on NFL.com

❋ A stomach that enters the room before he does

❋ His friends, two pounds of sour cream, and a wide-screen TV

❋ Graduation from Home Depot's "Lay Your Own Gas and Electric Lines" seminar

❋ More than one nonworking vehicle at any one time

❋ Finding Little Debbie snack wrappers jammed into the pillows of a chair

❋ A riding lawn mower with modified motor, customized faux fur seat, and horn

❋ Downloading behind a locked door

❋ Las Vegas and maxed out

❋ Beer cans, plumber's butt, and your parents

LOVE-NO ROUNDUP

Learn to use no with your husband without sacrificing your dignity or yourself. Never nag, and never screech. Merely speak from the place of the power of no, and use it to shape the relationship. He'll soon know what gives you pleasure as well as what you'll accept, what you'll merely tolerate, and what you'll blow him out of the water over.

From refusing to launder his "Say No to Drugs, Say Yes to Me" T-shirt to a "maybe later" when he invites you to Home Depot to check out the new Awesome Auger with six dirt-blasting attachments, no will take you through the arc of love from first glance all the way through the anniversary where you get your picture in the paper. So remember:

* "No."
* "No, baby."
* "No way, baby."
* "Not if you were the last testosterone-toting vessel on earth."
* "Maybe."
* "Maybe later."
* "Maybe next week."
* "Not tonight."
* "We'll do it on the way back."
* "Sure, if you spend the weekend at my mother's."
* "I'd love to. But I can't."
* "No. I just can't."

* "No."

* "Fine."

* "That's fine."

* "Do what you want."

Or, try entering one of his fantasies and dash his hopes there, the old **yes-no** thing:

* "Riiiighhht, dude. And I'm Pamela Anderson."

CHAPTER 3

GETTING BY WITH A LITTLE NO FROM MY FRIENDS

No in Friendship

While husbands require you to say "No more personal electronics this month" and "I disconnected it because no one can watch eight games a day" repeatedly, the **friend no** is like a snowflake: No two are the same. Friends are fat, thin, short, tall, old, beautiful, smart, funny, slow, sly, young, and ugly. They are intriguing and satisfying, and no amount of money is worth a one of them. Friends are life.

Friends fall into many categories: friends for life; friends forever; occasional friends; regular friends; friends of convenience; and the ever-perplexing friends you don't really like that much but they're, well, *friends.* Most people past the age of three have a vast, complicated net of friends, some that will remain in their lives forever.

We agonize over everything from the spouse's Mountain Dew habit to how to manage the boss's personality. We would never deal with a mother-in-law by the seat of our pants. So why don't we spend much time pondering how to keep friendship steady? After all, what are friends for? You should be able to be yourself—the good self as well as the one that draws and quarters a waiter for forgetting to leave the ice out of your ice water—and your friends should just plod right along with you, loving you each step of the way.

*It takes a great deal of bravery
to stand up to our enemies,
but just as much to stand up
to our friends.*
J. K. ROWLING

Well, think again.

Here is a snippet of conversation between my friend Rebecca and a waiter: "This lamb, where is it from? Australia, you say? I was hoping for New Zealand. Hmmm. How about the chicken? Free-range? But what if I want it without the citrus sauce? Oh, so that's just grilled chicken. How do you cook your vegetables? Lightly salted water only, I hope—I have hypertension. Look at the price on the foie gras green apple gelée! With two children in college, that won't be seeing the inside of *my* stomach. . . . " So intense, endless, and, well, personal is this exchange over what to order, I find myself having shame attacks as if my mother were telling my first-grade teacher I taught school to the family Scottie. (Her name was Bon-Bon, and she sucked at math.) So bad did this become—Rebecca's canoodling with the menu, me becoming itchy and enraged—that I had to figure out a way to shut down the dinner dance or not see Rebecca at mealtime, the only point in the day when I have time to see anybody.

In the end, I went for a full-frontal no that turned into **no negotiation.** After all, we have known each other since fourth grade.

"Rebecca, this psycho sex dance you do with restaurant menus has to stop."

"What do you mean?"

"It takes 10 minutes for you to cross-examine the waiter. Most times, he has to grill the cooks to answer your questions. Why don't you just go into the kitchen and make it yourself?"

"I have no idea what you're talking about."

"Next meal, you have three minutes, or we never go out again."

"What a bitch. I am not going to abide by your stupid rules."

Abide she did. Well, sort of. She's gotten it down to about five or six minutes and rarely asks what kind of soil sustained the basil.

STRONG FRIENDS SAY NO

Given the importance of friendship in the richness of life, it would behoove everyone to give it more thought and proceed accordingly. Given the number of situations where a lover or spouse will stand, squeal, and run from the room upon hearing your situation, you need your friends. I mean, how many times has your husband gone back with you to the salon that permed your hair into standard poodle land and helped you get your money back? How many times have you said "gynecological procedure" and your man jumped up and yelled, "I'd love to go!"

Friends will tell you yes when a lot of other people will tell you no. In the friends for life realm, anything goes, right? Well, usually it does, for these are the people that get you, love you pretty much unconditionally, and accept many of your stranger ways with ease and grace.

However, once in a while their lives and yours collide in

an unpretty way, and decades of tightness grow loose. Face it; there are times when you must explain yourself to your closest friends, saying no to their requests, needs, and schemes in both delicate and not-so-delicate ways. When friends of convenience become inconvenient, should they go? Should they stay? Should the connection change? And exactly how often do you say no to friends you don't like—such as your husband's weekend touch-football teammates, especially Jim, who yells "Take all my juices!!!" at any woman he sees? Or your sister's ex-boyfriend who still comes round because he can't quite believe your sister doesn't want him? How far should you go with your significant other's friends simply to keep peace in the land?

THE VERY, VERY CLOSE NO

A very close friend should be able to hear a no slide or shoot from your lips without feeling anger or hurt, right? Well, maybe. Endlessly nuanced, the friend no should fit the friend and situation as flawlessly as you can manage. Say this is a very close friend, a keeper. That doesn't mean he or she won't need a good noing from time to time; it just means that you should consider it carefully and land it perfectly.

A best friend just dumped by a four-year boyfriend doesn't automatically get to take your mate to a work event just to have an escort. Sharing men is rarely a good idea. A simple "I just don't lend him out" should end the discussion. Okay, so what about clothes? Lend a T-shirt, but if you let her take an evening gown, especially when her behind sticks out a bit farther than yours, you're asking for it. You can say, "Girl, your butt is way bigger than mine, and you are gonna stretch that dress to hell and back." But I recommend "I don't lend it out" here as well.

While some people are blessed with a close friend who accepts "no, jackass" without rancor, most folks need more tender care. Think deeply about what your friend is really asking and most times you can happily comply. But if you want a profound friendship to stay that way, protect it. Why would you ever jeopardize a wonderful girlfriend over something as transient as a man or a dress?

NOT SO PLEASED TO MEET YOU

Acquaintances sometimes become friends. But more often, they stay on the outer edge of life, sometimes bringing pleasure and sometimes bringing the same, allover itchy feeling as certain synthetic fabric blends. These are the people who call about serving on committees, helping with fund-raisers, inviting you to large mixers where time passes as it did for American soldiers on the Bataan death march during World War II. The acquaintance is not as dangerous as, say, a neighbor nor as complicated as a friend; polite noes usually send them scurrying. Again, the

53

more time you give an acquaintance, the less time you have to give to someone you truly love. Or to a nice, long, hot bath, for that matter. Think carefully. Do not fall into the trap that to "belong" to a community of any sort, you must serve more established members of that community willy-nilly. This is your life, remember?

Don't fall for someone like Margaret, a woman of incredible prestige and community gravitas, who often assembles committees for a world of good works. Her most difficult task is to gather the poor women to address invitations, which usually number in the hundreds or even thousands. These poor "volunteers" sit around a long table, hands cramping into claws, not unlike slaves rowing in the galley of a slave ship. All dream of promotions to the sign or flower committees. Few make the cut. For every time Margaret fills a committee of envelope addressers, she throws down her half-glasses and throws up her hands, crying, "Thank God for social climbers!"

A LITTLE HELP WITH YOUR FRIENDS

Because friendships are, hopefully, long and sometimes complicated, they take a very special **no mojo.** Be at your most thoughtful. While sometimes a no is launched to offend, the friend no is often a way to draw one closer and deepen an understanding between two people. Here are a few examples of the nuances between the friend no and the **regular old no no.**

To a friend who invites you and your kids to Inuit theater at the local art museum in an effort to explore as many cultures as possible: "Elizabeth, I can't imagine what this could be about besides fur, seals, and marine mammal fat. I think your curiosity is terrific, but the very thought of it makes me want to jump in my kayak and paddle behind the first ice floe I see."

To a drunken friend who has asked your husband to dance repeatedly one Saturday night: "You dance with him again, and you have to take him home and feed him. And, believe me, that ain't easy and that ain't cheap."

To your perfectly sober best friend who called to change a lunch date for the third time: "Emily, buy a damn calendar. Use it."

55

CHAPTER 4

I DIDN'T TOUCH YOUR TUPPERWARE

No at Work

In love, friendship, and marriage, no can be murmured, blurted, and sometimes shouted with desirable results. Work, however, is a completely different animal. At work there are bosses, clients, colleagues, and shareholders. There are vendors to whom you look to give you a good price and good service. There are security guards whom you rely on to let you into the building off-hours. There are operators who screen the completely mad from your phone. In short, the workplace is a complex ecosystem, and you must manage the flora and fauna with the utmost care. And that means no direct noes.

Think of Richard Nixon, accused at the beginning of his career of taking money from rich supporters. He went on television and turned his criminal behavior into a tale of woe about his kids and their little dog Checkers, a gift: "I want to say right now that regardless of what they say, we're going to keep it." Wow. We didn't expect him to say "yes, I did it," but we really did expect a "no, I didn't do it." In the end, this fiendish genius of a public manipulator made us feel badly because someone wanted to take back his children's dog when he was taking money he wasn't supposed to take.

Not only do businesspeople not want to take a fall, they don't want to quash what might be a really good, lucrative idea. More precisely, they don't want to be the ones perceived as saying no to moneymakers. Imagine Henry Ford saying, "I want to make these thingamajigs with wheels, and we'll all climb into them and move around, and it will be very cool," and someone in his company jumping up and yelling, "That's ridiculous!" Well, you just don't want to be that someone.

The **work no** is part diplomatic splendor, part verbal contra dancing. Unless you are a president in your second term, do not use the Harry "the Buck Stops Here" Truman method of calling 'em as you see 'em. Take my word for it: The average American business is less concerned with truth than were the leaders of Argentina in the 1970s and 1980s. Work is the place you get things done: Pretend it's thrilling, satisfying, and deeply, personally rewarding; and never, ever say a direct no to anyone, from colleague to boss. Work is the place where when you want to say, "This work is undoable crap and you are trying to make me look like a fool," you say, "This is a special challenge for a motivated, proactive person, which I am."

And don't be fooled again: No one really knows the meaning of the word *proactive,* especially people who use it a lot. It's a nonsense word, like *snickerdoodle* or *gewgaw.* Once you hear the word *proactive* at work, you understand that not only should you never use the word *no* directly, you should fold as many nonsense words as possible into everything you say.

Consider this.

You: I have a great idea for making this whole process easier and clearer for everyone.

Your boss: Okay, kiddo, give it a look at 30,000 feet and let me know what you find.

I may be presumptuous, but I don't think you know how to fly. Thus, your boss has delivered a nonsensical phrase that means, at the very least, "Stand down and leave me be" and, at the very most, "You fool, why would we want to do this faster and better? What will we do then? More work?!"

> *I could have stayed home and*
> *baked cookies and had teas.*
> HILLARY RODHAM CLINTON

The boss meant no, but in the Never-Never Land of American business, he or she obscured it with metaphors suggesting speed, strength, aerodynamics, and the eyes of an eagle. You've been flattered and splattered like a bug on a windshield at the same time.

In business, you must learn not only to tart up your no into something that feels like a yes or, at the very least, a maybe, you must learn to translate the well-disguised no and act accordingly.

GETTING THE JOB

By all accounts in the eyes of the "experts" who write business books, you are not in a no position during a job search. But listen: You will spend more time at that job than with your husband, companion, family, friends, and pets combined. If you make the mistake of yessing the first thing that comes along, you may inadvertently plunge yourself into a fiery hell where you will be tied to a rock and, rather than have your liver pecked out by a giant bird for eternity—a much-celebrated myth of yore—you must execute pointless task after pointless task while unintelligent people yammer at you. (I once had a job inputting phone numbers that existed in another database but had to be reentered because the company was too cheap to buy programs that could speak to each other—all the while, the woman next to me told me day in and day out about her surgery "down there.")

If your creditors call you more than your mother does, by all means, take the first job you're offered, still the endless ring of the phone, and pay some bills. Then start really looking.

A **great no position** comes when you interview for a job that is not the job you have now. While inside you may be screaming at the interviewer, *Save me from those idiots I work with now and their endless nits and their smelly reusable, resealable, plastic "I'll bring my lunch in this thing" things,* do not let it show. You have a job; you're covered.

For, unlike the last century, when tenure at one job could last a lifetime, employers today expect you to be on the move. They expect that you will always be looking for another, better job. And if you are not living up to their expectations, you need to start.

Everything nourishes what is strong already.
JANE AUSTEN

Ask a potential employer the tough questions. If the salary is not what you expect, state the number you need and tell them, "This salary is below my expectations and not enough to entice me from a job I love." Oh yeah. You've told them you are valuable because others value you. You have told them you love your work. But what you have really told them is no.

Understand the market for your skills and your worth. Just as you waited to return the call of a potential date despite your internal loop of *Me want him!* you must make the potential employer wait despite the "I'll take it!" burning unsaid on your tongue. You must remind the potential employer that you have choices, and choices mean a very real potential for no.

If and when they finally offer you the job, thank them professionally, and say that you need to assess your career options—the professional equivalent of "I'm no tart"—and will let them know. If they demand an answer in 24 hours, ask for 48.

Remember, you are dealing with businesspeople, and businesspeople are wired for competition and negotiation. The more you make them feel you are wanted elsewhere, the more they will want you with them. And that means a more successful negotiation for salary, benefits, and that extra week of vacation we all so desperately need.

That means a future with the promise of respect.

NO AND THE BOSS

The boss never gets a full-frontal no or even a vaguely negative reaction. The boss really can't take it, and, believe me, he or she will hold it against you. Of course, if it's sexual, the gloves come off, and no is delivered with extreme prejudice. But odds are your no won't be aimed at fat, groping fingers. Usually it's something just plain stupid. Whatever your boss does, let it slide, verbally dance around it, and turn it into a good story later.

> *Meet the new boss*
> *Same as the old boss.*
> PETE TOWNSHEND

NEVER DO THIS

On a business trip to a prestigious East Coast medical school, Lisa was standing at the boarding gate, ready to fly home. Her boss, a woman with helmet hair of great renown, wore a gray wool suit, a long strand of pearls, and a mink thrown over her shoulder. Apropos of absolutely nothing—they had been discussing an outlet mall outside of Philadelphia—the boss says, "You know, I have a good friend who is leaving her husband because she cannot stand the smell of his balls." Lisa did not miss a beat: "I always check that out first when I'm dating someone new." What Lisa did not say was "You are never to talk about testicles in my presence again." She had to play along, as the boss must never, ever be told "No, stop saying that, don't do it." But Lisa was powerless for only a short time:

She's elicited many a human scream when she's since told this story over cocktails.

WHAT?

Great tracts of American business have been infested with MBAspeak, a language peppered with meaningless sports and thriller metaphors—and even less meaningful word sequences—which, added together, have created a corporate illiteracy unprecedented in the history of organized human endeavor.

> *Employee:* I believe that if we turn the packaging into a self-mailer, it could really revolutionize our business.

> *Boss:* Why don't you go ahead and run the bases on that one?

Was that a yes? A no? A yes-no? So devoid of meaning was the boss's response, it can only be viewed as "You wanna open that can of worms? Fine. But you'll get no commitment or guidance from me."

To succeed at your job (not necessarily to please the boss or be liked, which are completely different things), you must learn to blast through the rubble of useless words.

> *Boss:* Why don't you go ahead and run the bases on that one?

Employee: Okay, Jack. What exactly would you like me to get you—a full proposal with budget projections? Input from sales and marketing? When would you like me to have it ready?

You have not said, "No, Jack. I'm not going to run the bases on that. I'm going to do my job." You've not said a direct no to him. Nor have you accepted one of those endless nonsense responses in the workplace, words meant to delay, obfuscate, and generally confuse. If you say yes to that stream of strangely couched noes, you will never get ahead. Because getting ahead is about generating and executing ideas. Getting ahead is about blasting through the white noise of commerce and actually doing something. Getting ahead is about learning and bringing forward what you know.

65

Employee: I've checked with the warehouse, and it seems that, for some reason no one can yet figure out, every time we receive an order for the specially priced collection of *Think and Do* books, the computer says to ship *The Joy of Lesbian Sex.*

Boss: Whoa. Situation critical.

Do ya think? Here's the person, the boss—and I bet you it's a man—using Tom Clancy words to talk not about a Navy Seal operation but a fulfillment problem. Maybe he's got an idea of how to fix the situation . . . ? Maybe the next question you ask is just that. Because by not asking intelligent questions or offering solutions, the boss is saying, "Go away. You frighten me. You want me to do my job. *Nooo!*"

Sometimes meetings feel like someone is reading a commercial script for penile erection dysfunction medication.

> **Boss:** Beth, if the situation persists, call someone.

> *"If you experience painful erections or erections lasting more than four hours, contact the nearest health care provider."*

Who would that be? The Williamses next door? "Hey, come look at my husband's boner!" I mean, who am I supposed to call? The last health care provider that took an interest in me was a nurse practitioner fascinated with my rash that happened to take the shape of Oklahoma. In the case of a job situation, I would assume I should call my boss, just as in the case of a never-ending hard-on, I would think the drug company might have to answer.

> **Boss:** Beth, we thought it was time, but maybe it's not time. We're lucky. When it is time, we have the tools. We'll be ready.

> *"You mean, your wiener-stiffening meds have not kicked in yet? Why not now? How long are you going to talk like a penile erectile dysfunction commercial and not do your job?"*

All that any job offers you is the opportunity to develop so you can get your next, better job. *No,* the word in business that dare not speak its name, is coated with Willy Wonka layers of meaningless, sticky goo meant to slow or stop you. Chew on through.

THE BOSS IS, WELL, NUTS

Never act like a boss is nuts, and never, ever give her or him direct negativity. A no directed at the boss must be carefully wrapped in the prettiest of packages. If the boss asks for a report by 5:00 p.m., say, "Single- or double-spaced?" But also say, "That will push back the delivery of the numbers you wanted from me earlier." Not one no or "I can't" has slid across your lips. If the boss asks you to do an onerous, thankless task, point out that there are colleagues with more suitable skills. Say, "Boss, I'm flattered you thought of me for that. But I'm concerned about this aspect of the project and would love to observe someone with such-and-such experience do it first." Not only have you dodged the dreaded deed, you've helped your boss be a better manager.

Do not volunteer. Your silence should serve just fine as a no, unless you've thought it through and really want to do whatever it is. Why be on a silly committee that wastes your time and makes it harder to get done what you were hired to do in the first place?

Wait for something of note to take on as extra duty because all you'll get for doing everything is doing everything. The boss didn't get to be the boss by being a patsy and no doubt has trouble respecting those who are. Draw your lines respectfully, but draw them. Work hard, place value on your time and skill, and don't put weird homey furniture, hand-crocheted throws, boxes made of Popsicle sticks, or tiny handprints in a clay disc in the corner office when you get there.

Helpful Phrases When Working with the Boss

1. "You said next Thursday, didn't you?" Translation: "I don't want to do this ridiculous task, and if the boss doesn't remember when it's due, well . . . "

2. "I'm on it" or "I'm all over it." Turn the snickerdoodle kind of phrase to your advantage, and buy time during which the boss will probably forget what he or she requested or at least give you time to do what you were asked to do.

3. "Brilliant. You're brilliant." Works well. Give the boss encouragement when he or she actually gives you bossly ideas and feedback. They, too, are mammals and will respond to positive conditioning.

WHO *IS* THE BOSS?

If you are a boss and want people to excel at their jobs under your firm, wise guidance, you must learn to till the land before planting your no. Or, to use a coarser comparison, you need to plump them up and let them fly before you blast them out of the sky. Employees must be encouraged while being contained. This is no easy matter. Just ask Julius Caesar, Charles the First, and Richard Nixon. (And don't think, *They are dudes; of course they didn't know how to manage.* They are dudes because it is only in the last 20 to 30 years that nondudes actually got to do something besides wash, boil, and type.)

The most effective way to say no to an employee is to learn to say no without ever saying the word. The **no without no** is an 8.5 on the no difficulty chart, and it may take time to master its execution with little forethought and perfect precision.

The employee no without a no is somewhat like the boss's no: You never actually open your mouth, put your tongue on the roof of your mouth, and push out a no. But, unlike saying no to the boss, when saying no to underlings, you must always stay on higher ground. You must keep the advantage or you lose your bossy-ness.

It looks like this.

> *Employee:* I want to take our product and get it in the hands of famous people who will then mention it during interviews or write our product into scripts.

> *You:* That's a very interesting idea. But I'm not sure that's the business we're in, Billy.

Ah, the noness of that remark is breathtaking. You have flattered the guy, thus encouraging his future ideas. At the same time, you have told him that this idea, right now, is not only not doable, he might want to spend a few hours on the intraoffice Web site reacquainting himself with the company's products and purpose. *Ker-pow!*

INTRODUCE THE IDEA OF NO YOU

A brilliant writer and thinker at one of the world's most prestigious newspapers was made head of her department. At a large weekly meeting of both her superiors and the reporters she managed, chaos erupted. Egos flared. Voices rose, blame was laid, and there seemed no end in sight. This late middle-aged, impeccably dressed, graceful woman stood and yelled, "Who do I fuck to get out of this job?!"

The room went dead. In one short, loud, shocking question, the woman had introduced both her employees and her bosses to a world without her while turning the ridiculous "sleeping your way to the top" on end and hurling it upward. So extraordinary was this no that it has become a kind of urban legend of noness. But it apparently happened, and those who witnessed it said it was beautiful.

BIG CHIEF RUNNING BOSS

My elders taught me an invaluable tactic for saying no in the workplace without ever saying no—or anything at all, for that matter. Employees cannot ask for something if they cannot catch you. There are no raises, there are no dollars for pet projects, there are no sign-offs or thumbs-ups if they cannot find you, their boss, and ask. Work with your door closed. If you have to leave your office, grab a pile of paper, put a "glimpse of Armageddon" look on your face, and run down the hall. Take an important call. Or better yet, make one, even if it is to your dry cleaner. And don't tell me you're too mature for this avoidance technique. If you've been a boss for more than six months, I'll guarantee you've done it. Childish? Yes. Effective? You bet.

This technique is simply a time-honored stalling tactic that will allow an employee to think more deeply through the request. Often, he or she will see the pointlessness or impossibility of the whole affair, and the issue will never reach your desk. If it does, it will be more fully formed and plausible when you finally hear it. You've taught the employee an important strategy of the workplace—"think it through"—and saved yourself three sessions of gently guiding and cajoling the employee back out of your office and into his to figure it out. Employees can free-associate on their own time.

Spots where Chief Running Boss is likely to get jumped:

In a meeting that's breaking up. Hanging around a table or desk where a meeting has just been held and people are milling about saying things like "I'll call that guy today" or "My hair hasn't looked right since my wife left" is one of the deadliest spots on earth. It's Baghdad, the North Sea, and I-95 all rolled into one. *Clear the area immediately* or you will become the victim of "Hey boss, I was doing a little thinking in the tub this morning. . . . "

In the bathroom. They will certainly attack your flank as you pump liquid soap onto your hands, but it's not just at the sink that you need to worry. They will look under the stall door, identify your shoes, and talk to them. Yes, they will pitch your shoes if you aren't fast and clever enough. Through the course of your day, vary your bathroom habits. Stop in on another floor. Don't go right after lunch or right before you leave the office. Keep your employees off balance. This will help preserve your noes until they are truly needed.

NO AND THE CO-WORKER

You should think of your co-workers as members of your platoon, not members of your family. You are on a mission with these people; you watch each other's backs and provide cover in a firefight. Identify weak areas in the group: The road is paved with land mines, utter fools who will get stepped on and blow all over the place, taking you with them if they can.

There are no cease-fires, no demilitarized zones: the bathroom, employee snack area, and office Christmas party are full of enemies in full camouflage gear. They might look okay—comfy shoes and Sansabelt slacks or a nice wraparound skirt—

but they are on duty and dangerous. They are here to gather information that they will then drop in the boss's lap like precious flowers or bits of gold. They are here to weasel their way into your heart, play on your emotions, and get you to do some of their work.

Your most potent no to colleagues is simply a lack of availability. They cannot slough off work on you if you cannot be found. They cannot waste your time—thus keeping you from progress and achievement—with their inane tales of do-it-yourself projects or feelings about sporting events—if they cannot find your ears. And, should anyone try to soil you with unearned blame, nothing but a head-on discussion of who truly did the deed delivered into their faces will do. (Remember, vampires hate to be pulled out into the light.)

The world of co-workers is filled with time-wasters, gossips, fiddlers, complicators, manipulators, tattletales, butt kissers, obsessive-compulsives, the sloppy, and the foolish. There are also hardworking, highly intelligent, interested people in interesting jobs. Find them and work with them. It's like the adage in shooting pool and playing tennis: Play with someone who's got a great game. No to everything and everyone else.

NO AND THE CLIENT

If someone is paying you to do something, this person is somewhat like your boss and never, ever gets a full-frontal no. Clients get many, many weird, undoable, and just downright self-destructive ideas. Part of your job—a big part of your job—is to save them from themselves with ingenious flattery that is really a big fat no.

Client: Why are we using professional actors? Why can't I be the one in this commercial?

You: I've watched you. I know you are a genius on camera. But I fear the public might associate you with the oil spill, creating a less positive image as we develop you and your company's ideas and products in the future. Could we focus on filming cleanup efforts now and use you for the next one?

As the universe would have it, this CEO was not around to appear in the next ad, but this account executive brilliantly avoided disaster with nothing but good old-fashioned butt kissing, a well-camouflaged weapon in the no war.

Clients come in many sizes, from those big, all-consuming ones that pay the salaries and keep the lights on to the small, all-consuming ones that you don't know who let past security. Know the difference and gauge your no accordingly. If a big client calls so often you haven't been to the bathroom in six hours, try "Jim, you are giving me so much great info that I fear something will get lost. Could you do one big e-mail at the end of each day with all your great ideas so I don't miss a step?" And for pesky little ones, there is always "Bob. Bob. I need to get off the phone and wait for your next call."

(This last quote has been attributed to a much-celebrated director of a book publicity department who was being stalked by the authors of *No Fat Mexican Cooking*.)

GADGET REHAB, OR THE DARK SIDE OF THE BLACKBERRY

The BlackBerry (and every other portable communication device, past or future) can be a portal to woe. If you think you work too much now, spend too much time managing the anxiety of your boss, employees, clients, and customers, what is that BlackBerry going to do to your Friday night? What does Sunday morning feel like as you sort through the often chemically compromised "deep thoughts" that those you do business with had on Saturday night?

Until you are very strong and powerful (no matter what position you hold), you must say no to the BlackBerry. That doesn't mean you shouldn't get one—you just need to turn it off at night and for most of the weekend. You own the technology; it doesn't own you.

Just because someone pays you money for honest work, it doesn't mean they have access to you off-hours (unless you've been dumb enough to go work in politics or entertainment).

76

Establish the BlackBerry no—"Boss, I won't respond until Monday unless this is an Enron-type thing"—and stick to it. Don't fall for your own attention deficit disorder and spend four hours of a Saturday in fractured, pointless smoke signaling to a colleague or client. You are not connected; no one is going to value you more because you'll answer lonely electronic peeps all weekend. No one thinks, *I can't downsize Sue! She's a great late-night e-mailer! When I can't sleep or let go of anything that's ever happened to me, I can send a message to Sue!*

Is it them or is it you? There is communication, and there is ever-spiraling-out-of-control compulsive-obsessive digital pecking that has more to do with addiction than reaching out. If you can't say no to your electronics, **gadget rehab** may be in your future. Imagine the shame.

USING NO TO GET TO YES

Every negotiation begins with no. If it didn't, it wouldn't be a negotiation. Someone wants something that the other is not willing to part with or not willing to part with without getting something in return. And some say that every aspect of business—or, for that matter, every part of life—is all negotiation.

Whatever the proposition, whatever the service, if you are the buyer rather than the seller, you'll get double or triple the service or goods if you play hard to get. If you are the seller rather than the buyer, deliver the message, then wait. Be patient. Don't pay attention to the cajoling and the tears. Wait to hear what you want to hear, then—and only then—say yes. Or even just maybe. Wait for the deal to be the way you want it. If you aren't experiencing success, say no and move on to the next competitor.

Being a capitalist means never having to say yes.

CHAPTER 5

FOUR WALLS TO HEAR ME

No at Home

If you look at all the areas of life where you cannot say no aloud, places where much is out of your control, why would you ever allow anything in your home that disturbs, disrupts, antagonizes, and annoys? Or at least allow it for very long. Home is where the heart of no is: Do not let things you don't like in here. (That means gangs of teens. That means raccoons trying to get in the dog food. That means blaring television sets. That means huge lumps on your couch that don't move for what seems like days.)

Rigging your house for no—known as **interior no design**—is an important part of **your noness.** If you live alone or with others, you must have a room that is your kingdom, your solace, your joy. This means no visitors unless invited; no input on the decor; no breach of the doorway; no touching of your stuff; no peering in the window.

Whatever you do in this room of your own is completely up to you. It could be an office, a dressing room, a library, or a bathroom with bubbling tub. It can be a converted garage, a finished basement, or a corner of the porch. But everyone that comes within its reach must understand: This space is yours, with no exception. This is the place where you do what you do and think what you like or stare agape at a wall. This is a place where you can work, nap, daydream, and ponder. All creativity needs room to take shape (and if you don't think putting together a satisfying life takes much imagination and even more elbow grease, think again). And if the whole world is yapping—buzzing, beeping, ringing, and screaming around you—odds are, you ain't going to get it together in a way that lasts.

In addition to creating physical space, you must learn to carve out psychic space, saying no to those trying sneak under your door via electronic blips, satellite reach, and good old-fashioned direct mail.

You own your computer, BlackBerry, and cell phone. You are their master. Must every blinking light and ringing phone be answered? Of course not.

You can choose to live in a world where a phone call can go to voice mail and an e-mail sits in the in-box to be answered tomorrow. You can choose to live in a world of your making—

not every call is important, not every beep needs immediate action.

Until you master that philosophy, don't turn on your personal e-mail in the morning: You'll be its slave all day. It's easier to send a polite no later in the day, perhaps even as your correspondent sleeps. **Noing voice mail** late at night or early in the morning may be a tad cowardly, but you sure will avoid awkward silences. The cell phone has caller ID for a reason; the ground line, a plug. Pull it if you really need to tell the world no. Personally, I wouldn't take the time to get myself off promotional mailing lists: Pick your noes carefully, and do not waste time noing something you can put in the recycling bin.

81

CREATING A HOME IS ABOUT CREATING TIME

To a great extent, the pleasure and peace of a home is created through your control of passing time. At work, huge forces—seen and unseen—set the speed at which many things are done. At home, you do it.

> *Remember that as a teenager*
> *you are at the last stage of your*
> *life when you will be happy to*
> *hear that the phone is for you.*
> FRAN LEBOWITZ

Robin grew up in a house full of ticking clocks, "yet no one would pick up a ringing phone," she says. "It took me a long time to understand that they loved the old clocks and loved the sound of the ticking. But the ringing phone wasn't necessarily about them. It went to the machine until they were good and ready to deal."

When Robin was a teenager longing for the phone to ring for her, she hated that no one picked up. "If my boyfriend called and I was out, tough noogie." However, as she got older, she began to appreciate the incessant ticking sounds and even the birdsongs that chirped from the Audubon clock that Robin's mother loved. There was a method behind the madness: If there are noises that drive you crazy, drown them out with noises you like.

Quiet and decelerate your home. Your nervous system, which has nowhere near evolved to match the demands of present technology, will thank you.

If you don't like the sound of a phone, adjust the answering machine to pick it up after the first ring. Check when you choose. That's why you have it, right? If you have a sudden, inexplicable terror that China is about to invade the United States, turn off CNN. Feel like al-Qaeda is sneaking up the back walk? Put the dog out and shut down the 24-hour news cycle. Fido will dispatch insurgents as your neurons recover from overuse.

Say no as often as possible to anything in your home that interrupts a smooth, as-peaceful-as-you-can-make-it passage of time.

NO HOME

Depending on your age and temperament, you'll sometimes think, *I'd rather be consumed by fire ants than go home.* If you need action, put on your cha-cha heels and go out! But if you find yourself noing your own home with frequency, well, something is up. Home should be the place where you can be completely comfortable and utterly yourself; a place that pulls on you no matter where you are. If you don't feel that way, you'd best begin to identify why and start noing it. If people are your trouble, start talking to them. If your bedroom is too dark, change the curtains and buy another lamp. Spend 10 bucks on flowers every once in a while, and for heaven's sake, keep the place clean. Money does not make a home, you do. And without a place where you can say no to the world, you truly are out in the field alone with a big hungry bird circling overhead.

> *The best thing I have is the knife from Fatal Attraction. I hung it in my kitchen. It's my way of saying "Don't mess with me."*
> GLENN CLOSE

DON'T TOUCH MY STUFF

Stuff touching is a **major no-no.** Perhaps you grew up with siblings who were always swiping your clothes. Or you had parents who, in the name of keeping you safe, constantly went through your private notebooks, diaries, and e-mail. Well, there is a difference between taking and borrowing, a line between concern and snooping. If you want your coinhabitors to respect your belongings, respect theirs. Know what possessions you feel strongly about and what you're willing to share. If you want to be asked about something particular, say, "You can wear that if you ask me first." You can also say, "If I ever catch you in my wedding dress in the neighbor's garage again, I'll take a picture and post it on the Internet."

Just because you live with someone you love doesn't give them the right to eat all the Chunky Monkey after you've expressed that the only thing that got you through the day was the thought of that ice cream when you came in the door. No matter how loving a person feels, eating another's frozen treat is selfish. And if someone does it to you, tell them no, don't ever do that again as they leave to go to the store and replace what they ate.

If your idea of intimacy is a total merging of feelings, thoughts, and stuff, by all means, let him read your letters to your college boyfriend. But you are allowed to have secrets, baggage from the past, places where you go alone. You are allowed to have possessions that are especially charged with meaning or, for whatever reason, highly prized. There is *your* stuff, there is *their* stuff, and there is *our* stuff. Know the difference and no the rest.

THE SOUND OF NO

Beyond space and stuff, sound is a common source of contention in a home of more than one inhabitant. There are times when everyone is doing the same thing. More often, people march to their own drummers and chase their own bliss. These are rarely silent activities. However, iPods have made blaring stereos obsolete. There is a "silent" setting on most personal electronics. The last two seasons of *America's Next Top Model* can be put on a computer and watched in private. One can actually look at a cell phone and see it light up rather than having it ring, vibrate, buzz, rock, and rap. Answering machine technology is advanced, and not only is screening calls acceptable, it is necessary. (Credit card companies will call before a payment is due, just another friendly service you get with your 21 percent interest rate. Or they might be offering you payment insurance, reminding you on a Saturday morning at 10:13 that you could be downsized at any moment.)

Buy clocks without a tick and machines that hum, not grind. Before renting or buying a home, find out if the windows seal out street sounds. Take a moment to listen to refrigerators and air conditioners. Again, to boost your neurological function, find a way to no noise in your home. (My husband hates the sound of a running commode. He walks the floorboards, head cocked, listening for the sound of water. I call him the Toilet Whisperer. Not to his face, of course.) The world has become one big boom box; you need a break.

NO STRANGERS IN THE HOME

From the plumber who leaves the job half done to the chatty mailperson, the home must be protected from the ruthlessness of strangers, and none are stranger than contractors.

Forget reality television, where polite, endlessly creative people who feel good about themselves show up and redo your house while you go to Applebee's for lunch. No one plays a mind game like a contractor. No one is more skilled at abandonment, double-talk, backpedaling, and all-around smoke blowing up the butt like a person you hire to come in your home and make it better.

Where did the plumbers and two assistants go? Well, from the pile of beer cans you discover next spring, they found a crawl space under the house where they avoided detection, caught a buzz, and did not plumb a thing.

What does "we'll be there next Tuesday" really mean? At the moment, it probably means "we intend to come here and work next Tuesday." But it also means "unless another, pricier job comes up" or "unless we mess something up on another job and have to fix it before the basement fills with water," then "we'll be there next Tuesday."

Here are some ways to fire a no at a contractor who has not yet learned who he or she is dealing with.

* "If you don't return tomorrow, I'll sue you."

* "You'll get the rest of your tools back as soon as you finish."

* "You'll see more money when I see the green paint."

* "Step away from the door; you are not leaving until this job is done."

* "When you arrived, there were no Mountain Dew, Ballantine, or Red Bull cans. There were no cigarette butts, McDonald's wrappers, or water bottles. They go with you, or you don't go." (And, if the project required the moving of earth, be extravigilant. These folks love a good landfill.)

From yard mowers to master electricians, no must be in play almost constantly to draw big dark lines around what exactly is required of contract workers for you to actually open your checkbook. This point of contact between you and the legion of plumbers' butts wanting to part you from your money is ground zero in the war at home. Tell them no constantly, and get what you want in writing.

NO AND THE EXTERMINATOR

If you don't believe that dealing with contractors is a life or death matter, consider this: An older couple lived on ranch land outside Dallas and noticed a baby rattler asleep in the sun in their front yard. Being experienced Texans, they knew a little rattlesnake probably meant some big rattlesnakes. So they called the snake guy, the rural Southwest's version of the urban bug dude. After a walk around the house, this intrepid exterminator said, "Yup. You've got snakes." The couple left for the day so he could commence his dirty, dangerous work. When they returned, he reported that more than 30 snakes, now dead, had lived under the house. He climbed in his van, a cocky sidewinder killer, and began to back out of the drive.

> *Richard doesn't really like me*
> *to kill bugs, but sometimes I*
> *can't help it.*
> CINDY CRAWFORD

"Did ya git 'em all?" yelled the homeowner.

"Probably!" he yelled back.

Needless to say, this aging couple sprouted wings and flew behind the van, risking bodily harm to say no to the exterminator's exit. When it comes to snakes, *probably* is just not a good word.

Know what the exterminator uses to exterminate. While it kills cockroaches or moths, your dachshund might also end up on its back with its legs in the air. And for goodness sake, don't let the exterminator slither off until you are sure what you wanted whacked is whacked!

REVENGE GARDENING

The backyard, deck, or tiny square of concrete where you put pots of basil can become a point of great contention with neighbors. You can become embroiled in the strangest of pissing matches, from a growing you-don't-know-why-their-brightly-colored-fake-toadstool-with-enormous-spots-enrages-you-but-it-does situation to a case like that of a man who actually shot down a dolphin-shaped wind chime. ("The pleasant tinkling enraged me," he told police.)

There is truth in the saying that "fences make good neighbors," and you should be ever vigilant about encroaching bushes, trees, ceramic animals, elaborate Christmas and Italian street-festival lights; seafaring pleasure craft and RVs parked out front; enormous umbrellas and inflatable yard objects; celebratory signs announcing births, birthdays, and "Go Colts"; and fountains with the water pressure of Ladder Company No. 4.

Because people are going to pretty much do what they want in their yards (and yes, it will often blow into yours), you need a strategy. Do not try to counter their bad sculpture with

a tasteful one of your own. Do not rush in and put a flowering quince in front of their poodle topiary. Tit for tat does not work in the garden. You must blot them out with long, interlocking materials in a wide range of delightful shapes, sizes, and textures. My father, a suburban warrior, loved rock. You may just want to go to Home Depot and buy something man-made.

THE LOVED ONES ARE COMING!
THE LOVED ONES ARE COMING!

Strangers are not the only threat to a home; you must protect yourself from the ones you love. Some live in other places and might want to come visit you.

Sometimes loved ones are clever. They say things like "Come visit! And of course you'll stay with us." You accept and sure enough, within six months, you can hear the roar of approaching jets, your recently visited relatives landing on their way for their turn with you. Or they'll call with tales of bright children, freshly spewed from college, yearning for adventure yet too poor to book a room. Who better to take them in, stimulate their minds, and offer them free room and board than you, the kindly aunt and uncle? Soon there will be clothes tumbling out of luggage onto the floor, food allergies that must be shopped and cooked around, and, God help you, phrases like "totally awesome" and "tickets for Ashlee Simpson" being bandied about.

If you accept hospitality of the bed-and-breakfast kind, you will be required to return it no matter what is going on in your life. The solution? Always make hotel reservations, and insist they make theirs. Not only will your house be cleaner, you will also be able to continue earning a living and have less chance of creating a rift in the family that lasts for three or four generations, at the very least.

The loved ones—family and friends—will usually approach you in three ways.

1. "I'm coming to town, and I can't wait to see you. I want to spend all the time with you I can!" Be delighted. Don't ask them where they are staying. As we learned earlier, saying nothing is a powerful, potent form of no.

2. "Can you recommend a good hotel for me to stay in?" Don't flinch when they set up that shot. Have a list in the bedside table drawer. Pull it out, put it forth, and offer to make the call and reservation on their behalf. Present a range from economy-priced to Ritz-Carlton–good. It is far better to be their travel agent than the one who has to launder every one of their damp towels daily.

3. "Can I stay with you?" They know you know that's what they were asking in the first place. But their urge to save on a hotel has driven them to blurt what the two of you have been dancing around from the start.

You must be brave. In order to thwart potential home invaders, never, ever tell them something that isn't true. Don't fire back with some wild invention about your work taking you to Beirut or a huge obstruction in your bathroom pipes that experts fear has, well, fur. You will be found out, and then you will be shunned. You don't want to lose valuable relationships over this, even if they are of the arm's-length variety.

So don't lie. But do fail to tell the truth—the truth being that you don't want them in your home or even that close to your home. Friends you step on as you shuffle to the bathroom in the middle of the night are often not friends much longer. Take them out. Show them a great time. Pay the bill. Wave good-bye.

When the phone rings, this is what you say: "Gee, I wish you could stay here, but I'm afraid it isn't going to work out." (Optional—but dangerous—words at the end of this sentence: *this time.*) This sentence will stop nine out of 10 yearning visitors in their tracks. What can they do? You have said no without saying no, and they are left to ponder what mysterious foreign mission or intimate circumstance separates their application for your living room couch from your hospitality.

And then there is always the 10th caller, the one with no shame who presses you about your lack of availability. Simply repeat that it "just isn't going to work out."

CHAPTER 6

C'MERE FOR A SECOND

No and the Family

As a person enjoying the middle part of my life (it's the cracking knees that I love so much . . . or maybe the way I sweat profusely in the grocery store for no apparent reason), I have certainly seen the effects of my inability to say no, especially to family. How many of us heard "You'll never be a lawyer!" or "You'll always be big boned!" or, my personal favorite, "Who is going to take you on?" in our formative years. Even the most loving of parents become exasperated and blurt hurtful things that, alas, we must spend a lifetime trying to work out of our bloodstream. I couldn't shout "No!" at the unkind words I heard at 12. But I sure can now. I can forgive and move on and never forget to have that little word handy to whip out like a revolver when a family member tries to squeeze off a shot.

OLD NO

Often in your home, you encounter family. Usually a good thing, it can go bad pretty quickly, especially with crafty older folk.

After a certain age, one must be very, very careful with parents and their seemingly harmless, tossed at you from the side, requests. You are grown, and your parents know it. They say things like "You'll always be my baby girl." They also wait for you to get full on their good cooking, rely on the fact you feel safe and comfortable, and then lightly let loose things like "C'mere for a second." When you do, they ask you to hold up a corner of the house.

My father, an octogenarian of some repute, lamented the condition of his yard vegetation, knowing full well it was the bait that would make me rise. He watched me trim these monstrous, fire ant–laced, prickly, brambly bushes at the front of his Texas ranch house. After hours of whacking and sweating and itching, I finished and asked my father to admire the job. He did not fail: "Looks neat! If you'd used the electric clippers, I know it would have been faster, but I doubt it would have worked out so nice."

Payback? Perhaps all the years of waiting up for me got the better of him, and he just couldn't help himself. He saw me out there with those low-tech tools, perspiring and grunting, and thought, *That is so fair.*

THE NOES OF OUR FATHERS

The ability to understand and effectively use the word *no* is learned, like tying shoelaces and telling time. My father used silence and carefully timed departures to great effect when he wanted to say no. My grandmother, who was quite fat, literally sat on things she didn't like. (I am still haunted by her plopping down on Bon-Bon.)

My brother used toads and night crawlers to define his "boundaries," and my mother—oh, my mother—was a true Mistress of No. Her noes were quiet, made of metal, and the remembered sound still makes my heart beat faster.

One of my mother's colleagues came visiting for the first time—a fellow teacher who happened to be black—in Texas—in 1974—and went next door to the wrong house. The neighbor glared through the door, screamed "What do you want!" and waved a shotgun at her. And her six-year-old daughter. I will never forget my mother softly dispatching the neighbor, the gun, and half the police force from our front yard, a no that has been burned in my brain and influenced much of how I feel about what is right and wrong in life.

Reach back into the **family no.** While I don't suggest you wave a toad at your husband when he "just checks a score" during your favorite show, you can learn from the noes of your mothers, brothers, sisters, and fathers.

NO AND LITTLE CHILDREN

I decided to say no to children in the big way so I wouldn't have to spend all day saying no to them in a million little ways. I said no to having my own kids so I could say yes to other people's kids. Unqualified to speak as a parent, I can only give advice in an Auntie Mame kinda way. And if you have your own children, that's of little use. So I suggest that if you are having trouble saying no, consult some of the great books on the subject. I can recommend two. The first, written by a college friend, is called *Yes, Billy, the Monster Will Eat You If You Go in There,* and the other is by my brother—a book for the parents of teenagers called *Are You Sure You Look Hot in That?*

NO AND BIG CHILDREN

Your once-young brothers and sisters, comrades in the campaign against parental tyranny, grow into people who, now large, can lose some of their shine. Fresh-faced siblings can go on to become drunk dialers, serial marriers, chronic money needers, and true screwups. Now, while you hear an adult voice pleading with you on the phone, your mind conjures a young, rosy-cheeked face that had the ability, years ago, to send you into "I just wet my pants" laughter.

Whether just-annoying-sometimes or actually sinister,

grown brothers and sisters can be as clever and dangerous as octogenarian parents.

You may fall for "Help me change the oil in my car—it'll just take a second." Hours later, covered in unspeakable goo with sidewalk burns down your back, you realize you've been had. But asking you for another $10,000 for a third divorce is not cute and funny like, say, putting a worm in your lunch box. Like everyone in your life, siblings need to hear no, too.

Get over your soft spot: "We're blood!" goes only so far. You are not an ATM and, while you would truly rescue a family member in need, you are not a root vegetable just fallen from a truck. Being played is being played, regardless of the source.

If you cannot get over your sentimental feelings for a great kid grown into a questionable adult, you are what psychologists call an enabler. In the world of no, we call it something else: sucker!

I DIDN'T SAY YES TO THEM

It has been advised to "marry an orphan" if you want a life with some semblance of peace. However, mates often have siblings and, even worse, living parents, and no matter what you do, you experience in-law irritation.

In-law irritation can take many forms. One of the most prevalent is the mother-in-law's "You're not doing that right," which can be answered in two ways: "Then you do it" and "Right says who?" Another huge stress point is time, especially around holidays.

Coupling does not mean that you become the chew toy of everything in his family that has teeth. You are not a sacrifice to his ancestors; you are his mate. He has chosen you and placed you apart. And that means he doesn't leave you unguarded when beasts are about. He must be the **agent of no** that protects you from what is really his: his parents, his brothers, his aunts and uncles, his cousins and sisters.

"Too simple!" you cry! No, it's not. If you have married a person who cannot maintain distinct, productive relationships, you are in a mess. If he can't say no to his mother, then *he* has to go when she calls. You do not. He must tell his cousin that your backyard cannot hold a confirmation party (besides, they should have waited until you offered!) and deny his sister access to your phone for her late night around-the-world telecons. Your only job here is to no him. He must no the rest; they are his.

> *Why? Why? It hurts so much.*
> *Why me?*
> NANCY KERRIGAN

If he turns out to be a nonconfrontation man (which you really, really should have figured out before you married his butt), you must formulate the strategy and hold the line. "We can only come for Sunday dinner once a month. We spend one with my folks and two in our home—you know, the one you were so glad we moved into so there wouldn't be a chance we might live with you."

WHAT YOU DON'T KNOW CAN HURT YOU

Far-flung relatives sometimes fling themselves at you, usually over the Internet. Aunt Elva gives them your e-mail address, or they just peel it off a family blast from Uncle Frank. Suddenly, someone is writing to you as if they know you. They are familiar and chatty. They want you to come to Buck Snort, Tennessee, for a family reunion. Were you to fly there, it would take two days. Whoever these people are, it would not be a good idea for you to run off to meet them. Chances are, they are not in your life for a reason.

Richard was from an old, established Southern family that prized their ancestors, their bourbon, and their furniture. They spent a lot of time having cocktails, gossiping about dead people, and rearranging the living room. When a grandfather clock of great pedigree—it had survived the Massacre of Cherry Valley in the 1730s—was willed to a distant cousin who had married three times before the age of 21, some were startled. Sometime later, they were downright appalled when Richard had to go to Florida after her death to retrieve it—from a trailer in a nudist camp. Alas, it was no longer in the double-wide, and he had visions of this glorious clock bashed to splinters and fueling a nudie wienie roast.

If you decide to dip your toe into your DNA pool, be prepared for some hard swimming. You have no idea what you'll find in that water. If it's a family reunion, go for the day. Do not hand your phone number out to every second cousin like some dumb tart. An e-mail address is a tad safer; you can see what arrives and, if too horrific, add to your blocked list.

DON'T PASS THE GRAVY, SEE IF I CARE

At no time is the family more dangerous than at a happy holiday meal. Your sister has been waiting nine years to blurt out that it was you who took the car out that night. Your brother-in-law finds the first 30 seconds after Thanksgiving blessing the perfect moment to announce how good your butt looks in those pants. Your aunt is simpering over her collapsed cake, and your dad is wielding the electric carving knife. All he needs is a hockey mask and a tree around which to tie you. Nieces and nephews blubber, yell rap lyrics, play electronic games that scream and explode, and get ahold of the tiny marshmallows meant for the sweet potato casserole.

Yup, you're in hell. And you're not getting out for at least six hours.

Keep in mind that today is the day when feelings will be

hurt, resentments will bubble to the surface, accusations will be heard, tears will spill. You will listen to boring stories, perhaps drink too much, and, of course, eat way too much. In fact, you will try to self-induce a coma with the amount of pie you consume, but the sugar paralysis subsides, and there is Uncle Walter, just where you left him, pants pulled to his chest, nonalcoholic beer in hand. You will feel like a child even though you are 47 years old, or worse, you will have worked for four days for a meal consumed in less than a quarter hour.

The family holiday feast requires a kind of **John McCain no.** No matter how much they may torture you, you are not giving up anything but your rank and serial number. You will not rise to the endless bait and engage in an argument that should have taken place when you were 10. You are a soldier, stalwart, unflinching. This is neither the time nor place to engage in battle. Observe, retreat, reassemble, and attack later, when the enemy force is not so overwhelming.

CHAPTER 7

THE GLOBAL NO

No in Life

After dealing with the microcosm—the plumbers' butts and surly 17-year-old checkout girls—what about your relationship to the macrocosm? You know, the big stuff. What do you really owe the world?

Many feel that bomb blasts in another hemisphere have nothing to do with them . . . or at least until they go to fill their tank with gasoline. Others don't make the connection between every forest on earth being flattened and the strange infectious diseases they now, rightly, fear.

Globalism is not simply about losing telemarketing jobs to the citizens of Bangalore. Globalism is about the fact that there are so very many people on the planet that one makes a move over there and ripples travel, finally coming to slosh over here, in your kitchen sink.

We struggle with the force and unfairness of the greater world all the time. When the "captain" of the *Exxon Valdez* was outed as being drunk at the wheel when he wrecked an oil tanker and an ecosystem, I cut up my card and sent Exxon a letter telling them off good. Did it matter? To me it did.

But what do we do about the children in the Middle East, hit by shrapnel in their own living room? Or the newly made hurricane homeless in New Orleans being turned back across a bridge because a town "couldn't" help them?

These are deep, agonizing moments of being powerless to deliver a no. But this is where your **no patience** comes in. You wait, and you vote. You make donations to those working for change. You find something right next to you that needs helping, and you help it.

DR. STRANGE NO

Saying no to strangers isn't a big thing, right? Well, have you ever been approached by a young woman holding a baby in the rain and asking for money? Have you ever noticed an elderly person, obviously on the edge of exhaustion, behind you in line at the grocery? And if that car cuts in front of you in traffic, what is really at stake?

I have given money to a woman holding a baby in the rain and heard her walk up to the person behind me and repeat her fund-raising spiel verbatim. Did that mean that she wasn't going to use the money to get her and the baby out of the rain? That maybe the money I gave her and the baby will never in fact be used by either one of them? I don't know. I just know that I am glad I gave it to her—for my own sake as well as hers. For when a stranger asks for something, what do you really owe him or her? What's at stake?

More than you might think. An evolved society requires that its citizens both respect and assist one another. If someone wants to pull in front of your car in your lane, your response should be a laid-back yes. Yeah, that driver is probably a moron and a louse. But that driver may also be late for the hospital room of a loved one or the office of a much-needed employer. If you can give some money to the young woman in the rain, do it. You may avoid road rage in the first instance, and in the second, well, you never know when you are the thing, the angel on earth, that brings the message of possibility and hope to another human being.

NO MORE COFFEE

As you travel through the world, many strangers approach in the form of "service providers." But oh, how some don't want to provide service. Consider the retail clerk who doesn't want to sell you anything or the waiter who simply won't wait. For these unknown folks, the word *no* is always appropriate and should be used with the free, heavy hand of a dictator-for-life.

Jackie waited for hours to have her tire repaired and changed. She was half a mile down the road when she realized she hadn't been given her spare back. One U-turn later, she asked the mechanic for the tire.

"What does it look like?" he smirked.

"Well," Jackie said, "it's black and round and it has a big hole in the middle. Just like this one!" She walked over to a brand-new tire, threw it into the trunk, and jumped in her car, yelling at the window, "Thanks for all your help!" as she exited the lot.

What should you do if your pants return from the dry cleaner so stretched they could fit Shaquille O'Neal? How do you speak to the outsourced worker employed by your credit card company who calls you on Sunday at 9:00 a.m. asking for payment on a bill not yet due? How do you handle the salesclerk in the underpants department who immediately walks you over to the extra-extra large bin when you inquire about a thong?

Never forget: You are the one paying. You are the one that must be pleased. Vote with your feet, and lead with your money. Say no to bad service every way and every day. You can start out politely with a firm tone and well-considered words. Then get a little hotter. No, you shouldn't have to shout. Ask for the manager. Get what it is you want or move on. There are a lot of people who would be happy to take your money *and* have pride in the service they supply.

NO NUKES

Saying no can change the world. It is an act of civil disobedience that has long and effectively been used in the face of injury and injustice. "Hell, no, we won't go" was the anthem of protestors who did not want to shoot—nor want their country to shoot—Vietnamese. The British freed India from colonial rule after the entire country said no and went on a series of sit-down strikes. A young man stood in front of and stopped a tank in Tiananmen Square during a student protest. The exact moment of his **profound no** was filmed and broadcast everywhere, sparking world anger over human-rights abuses in China.

Life may not be that dramatic, but no is the right and honorable way to exercise your rights as a citizen. Yes, you have to pay your taxes. But no, you don't have to patronize a retailer who sells clothes sewn by seven-year-olds chained to a floor in front of a machine in Central America. The Bush administration refused to participate in efforts to slow and halt the rest of the world's no to global warming. Look into hybrid cars; say no with your next vote. Every day you are faced with countless opportunities to say no to the unfair, endless nonsense of this world. Sure, it's just little old you. But it's a really good start.

A WORLD OF NO

Much can be learned from how our friends around the world transmit the negative. Here's a little taste of the global no.

No..English

Nyet.. Russian

Cha...Zulu

Tla ....Cherokee

Nein...German

Neen, Zonder..Dutch

Khong...Vietnamese

Nein............Austrian (except for the Viennese, who say *yes* for *no*—scary)

Tidak, bukan ....Malay

Dah.. Apache

Non...French

Hindi/hindi po...............Tagalog (Philippines; second form to an elder)

Ne ....Czech

Chikimba ....Choctaw

Nie... Polish

Dooda	Navajo
No	Spanish
A 'ole	Hawaiian
Nope	Brigidian (Western Ireland)
Nem	Hungarian
Nie	Belarusian
Ez	Basque
Lela	Arabic (North Africa)
Non	Latin (Ancient Rome)
Mhai	Cantonese
Bu shi, zhe yang	Mandarin
Naw	Texan, Scottish
Lo	Hebrew
Aca	Kikuyu (Kenya)
Aniyo	Korean
Nakhayr	Pashto (Pakistan, Afganistan)
Oha're	Catawba
Não	Portuguese
Kala Kala	Tamashek (West Africa)
Nei	Faroese
Haa-ha'	Chechen

> *That woman speaks eighteen languages, and can't say No in any of them.*
> **DOROTHY PARKER**

A GESTURE OF NO

Shoe throwing .... Iraq

Bobbing the head up and down .... Greece, parts of the
(the way we indicate yes) .... Middle East

Finger wagging from side to side, ... Much of Europe
as close to the face as possible

Gunfire .... Parts of Brooklyn and
the Bronx; all of Texas

Chapter 8

THE GREATEST NO OF ALL

No Yourself

After all the potential boyfriends, sex partners, corrupt governments, husbands, friends, contractors, acquaintances, and strangers have been noed, there is now only one person left standing. While you have spurned bad behavior and thwarted those who wanted to suck your time, energy, and life out of you, you might still have one problem. That problem is you.

Ever looked carefully at a credit card bill? That little summer dress you bought—the one you didn't need and didn't have anywhere to wear, but fit perfectly and was so you—has, through the magic math of credit card companies, gone from a fantastic sale price of $89 to more than $140 by the time all the checks were written, envelopes licked, and payment-due dates met. Oh, what a feeling, standing in a dressing room in a piece of clothing made for you. It's a short leap in your mind to the perfect garden party on a warm summer day, and Mr. Delicious has appeared and is offering you some champagne and all his attention. Yeah, it's great to dream. But not if it's going to bite you in the butt later.

You have just paid a Saks Fifth Avenue price for what began as Banana Republic good luck. You let yourself get sloppy and disregard the universal law of credit card companies: 13 to 18 to 23 percent interest on every item you buy, on sale or full price, means they're rich and you're not.

Why couldn't you tell yourself no? Did you really think that there would never again be a dress that makes you happy? Did you really believe the myth "Buy the dress, and he will come?"

> *My weaknesses have*
> *always been food and men—*
> *in that order.*
> **DOLLY PARTON**

This is a moment that demands **self-noification.** No matter how hard, no matter what your mood, you must be able to see into the near future when the bill arrives. You must be able to project to the moment when you realize that not only do you not have the money to buy this dress, you will not have the money for months, thus dribbling little bits of money out the door until you've paid almost $140.

What are some of the other ways we seem unable to no ourselves and must pay later? Here's a very short list.

Cheesecake reality: Cheesecake has the same amount of calories whether eaten in the dark alone or with the lights on in front of thin friends.

Closing time: After many beers, that mole on his upper lip doesn't look so bad, but when you wake up with him in the morning, you can count every one of the gray hoary hairs sprouting from it. There are usually more than three.

Low-rise jeans: No one looks good in low-rise jeans except a skinny male, age 16 to 24. Why do you buy them? Is the urge to show your back fat and top of your butt crack to the grocery boy just too much of a rush to give up?

Imaginary weight loss: A pair of beautiful linen pants stretch tight across your ass, straining at the seams. You buy them anyway, with the unassailable knowledge that you will lose 10 pounds. In actuality, you won't, but you still wear them to the company party and split them in front of your entire management team.

Teetering on madness: Nothing is sexier than a four-inch stiletto on a sexy summer sandal. You will look like you stepped from the pages of *People* magazine, a leggy red-carpet minx who, unlike Michelle Pfeiffer, gets the heel jammed into the bluestone on the Richardsons' back patio. Luckily, Bob Richardson is an auxiliary firefighter and knows just what to do.

The perfection problem: Learning to say no to your own drive for perfection is a very good thing because you will never, ever be perfect. Not even close. You will experience moments of perfect love, perfect joy, and perfect rage. But they pass quickly and there you are, stuck in the imperfect moments that make a life: running back to the store for the milk you forgot, getting to work 10 minutes late, or waiting for the cable guy.

You will do everything that everyone asks of you and still someone will say, "I wish you had gone a little deeper with the numbers on your report" or "The cake was such a surprise! Yes, it could have been a bit moister, but it was yummy as it was." You will sweat and grunt and still not have the butt of a goddess. You will have a to-do list, kill yourself to get to the end of it, and still have a nice new to-do list in the morning. So what if there's a little spillover from the day before? Get over your own need to be perfect. You aren't and you can't be. So what if you snort when you laugh? Who cares about the jiggly stuff at the top of your arms? I certainly don't; it's part of why you are so funny and cool. (In moments of disgust at my husband, I often slap at my upper-arm fat, creating a violent jiggling in his direction. He doesn't know what it means, and neither do I. But the gesture feels right.)

> *There are magazines devoted to*
> *you feeling bad about yourself.*
> *There are millions of dollars*
> *going into the idea you*
> *have a fat ass.*
> MARGARET CHO

My **personal no problem** of the moment is peanut M&M's. So what, you ask? It's not like I'm taking on the backfield of the Dallas Cowboys while my husband is away doing missionary work. But those peanut M&M's have twisted me up. I spend money (a lot) on a personal trainer but still have a half-moon of dimpled fat on my lower abdomen. I sometimes sit at work, and, while in the middle of an intense, important phone call, I think, *I'll just pop by Duane Reade and get a bag when I hang up.* By not being able to no myself, I have allowed peanut M&M's to turn me into a wiggly-bellied woman zoning out on the phone. Those M&M's (peanut, not plain) have imprisoned me, and only a self-no can bust me out.

THINGS I CAN'T SAY NO TO

Corn chips; Internet shopping; cats; *America's Funniest Home Videos*; whipped cream; cheap sunglasses; my boss; naps; making prank phone calls (yeah, *still*); any movie with Johnny Depp (no matter how weird); makeup samples (even for neck-firming creams); peanut M&M's (but you know about that, don't you); Bernie's laugh; eating potato chips in bed; dumplings; celebrity cellulite exposés; a beach; Gap underwear; good gossip; the smell of a horse barn; shoe sales; telling my trainer his ass sags; great bath products; a dog's eyes; Roxy's potato salad; a man with a really good butt; manners; good listeners; mooning Ruth; clean sheets and freshly shaved legs; driving when a great song comes on; athletic men (and golf doesn't count); asking a male colleague if his suit comes in his size; Isabel and Fernando; funny men with big ears and big hands; Jo Jo; cheap purses on the streets of New York; YouTube; hot tubs; new lipsticks; massage; *Law & Order* reruns; a really good book; frosting; pedicures; Prince concerts; and, most important, a good laugh.

121

NO END

In the final analysis, using the word *no* is about time and how you manage it. Your time. And, if you add up all the little bits of your time, the sum total is something that is called your life. When you think about it that way, it changes things, doesn't it? You can either drive carpool every day for your friend who likes to go back to bed, or you can tell her—politely—no and use that time to run in the park or teach a kid to read.

Saying no is about fighting for your life, defending the time and space to live as you feel you should, not as others would have you do it.

Saying no is about generating respect and putting value on yourself that others will recognize and want.

Is it worth all the risked hurt feelings, sullen stares, and resentments that might possibly result from the use of the word *no*? Is it worth the strange stomach flutters you get before saying no to someone you've never noed before? Is it worth the difficult, uncomfortable post-no moments you might have to endure to make your life cleaner, freer, and more deeply yours?

Yes.

Yes, it is.

GLOSSARY

(IN ORDER OF FIRST APPEARANCE)

yes years:

A sad period of life, often in the first quarter, where you believe that if you say yes to everyone, they will like you.

no time:

The delay between the time a request is made and the no delivered. Sometimes you are granted no time naturally, as in "Please RVSP by December 3." At other times, the request is buried at the bottom of a hole covered with leaves, and you just bumble and tumble into it. In case of ambush, have a pat phrase that kicks in automatically and buys you some time before delivering your no. I use "*Whoa. I am really messed up. Exhausted.* I think it's the middle-aged thing. Can I tell you tomorrow?"

warm up your no:

The flip side of no time, this is a no that you can see coming a mile off. You've been pecked, pestered, blown off, or bored one too many times, and you are going to deliver a perfect no line before galloping into the sunset.

full-frontal no:

Also known as the walk-up no. This is a no-mistaking-it, full-in-the-face no said clearly and sometimes at great volume.

the naked brother:

A surprise that can derail any gig, no matter how good. When the naked brother appears, you must say no, regardless. The naked brother is the thing that cannot be tolerated, overlooked, or borne in a relationship or situation. Example: *When the boss asked me to redo that report, it's as if the naked brother walked in.*

no-date space:

The time you determine between seeing a person of interest that often reveals much about that person's character and emotional construct.

reverse no-date space:

When the person of interest controls the time between contact in order to determine just what you are made of.

ultimate date no:

Usually delivered in the early stages of dating. It makes clear that you do not want to see the onetime person of interest again but holds no rancor, as you simply haven't built up enough baggage to put much energy into your no. You just aren't into it.

no gone terribly wrong or **insane no:**

Usually a remnant of misguided childhood instruction. The best example is the young man whose parents taught him that no one should touch his penis without his permission. He grows up interpreting this lesson as "No one should touch my penis, not even someone I'm having sex with."

no purgatory:

May occur in the early phases of interaction with a person of interest. You decide that person is a complete boob but discover he really can, you know, get you going *down there.* Keep him around awhile for sex, but do not fool yourself into believing that he will change and become, well, not a fool.

125

person of no:

A life status achieved not by money or elected membership. A person of no has learned to use no effectively and freely, creating an aura of respect. It's perhaps tinged with a little fear, but it's better than driving carpool every day.

land your no:

Like a nimble 12-year-old gymnast from an Eastern European country, you should be able to land your no and scamper off the mat with your pigtails flying.

deep in his noness:
A man so intent on telling you no that he hasn't noticed you are grinning and hitting on the waiter.

absolutely not:
A hard-line, old-school, punishing-nun-teacher, mean-babysitter kinda no. Especially effective with boyfriends and husbands.

no fork in the road:
If you see the no fork in the road, take it.

fortress no:
Circle the wagons, pull up the drawbridge, log off, silence the ringer. Nothing gets through, especially embarrassing attempts at winning you back.

no date tool:
Any form of communicating the fact that you never, ever intend to see this schmeryl again.

no sweat:
The visible discomfort that appears on the face and the physical mannerisms of an amateur no-sayer. Body indicators include wiggling, scooting, sweating, and short barking sounds.

plutonium of no:
Bolting, running, heading for the hills, grabbing your pants and dashing, flying, or fleeing a situation or person that is beyond reason.

bolt point:
When the internal pressure of someone's ickiness outweighs the external pressure of propriety and you just take off running. The actual bolt can be handled in two ways: *explain and go* or *just go.*

ultimate no:
Usually a phenomenon of late-stage dating, the ultimate no is a strategy to get to the ultimate yes: marriage. The ultimate no is a game of chicken, and you must be prepared to lose.

no options:
Do not always rush to just any old no. Rifle through your options. Deliver the right no for the moment and the noee.

yes-no:
A sarcastic no delivered as a yes. Example: "Right. And I'm Pamela Anderson."

friend no:
Nuanced, sophisticated, and full of gray areas. Must be considered carefully before delivery to a friend.

no negotiation:

Often in close relationships, getting to no is an intense series of compromises and counteroffers.

no mojo:

A powerful force that allows a human to move through life with grace and style, saying no to twits, morons, manipulators, takers, and other useless folk. A person of no (see page 125) is full of no mojo.

regular old no no:

An ordinary, everyday way that most people have of uttering the negative that, in run-of-the-mill situations, works just fine. These are the "nahs," "nopes," and "uh-uhs," the workhorses of negativity.

work no:

Equal parts Henry Kissinger and Gloria Estefan, the work no requires diplomacy and hot dancing.

great no position:

A wonderful spot where you don't need to have a situation go one way or another, so saying no is pretty much stress free.

no without no:

Most often used in the workplace or with hypersensitive people, the no without a no is an 8.5 on the difficulty chart. Never can a word that even vaguely sounds like the word *no* be spoken. Some examples are "Interesting idea!" or "I'm not sure that's the business we're in, Billy."

gadget rehab:
The place you end up when you can't learn to say no to your cell phone, computer, iPhone, or BlackBerry. They put you in a room, take away your electronics, and make you write long, grammatically correct letters by hand.

interior no design:
A way to approach one's living space that affords the maximum amount of peace and tranquillity possible, as well as a guarantee that no one will touch your stuff.

your noness:
A facet of your deepest identity, your noness defines that crap you just ain't going to put up with.

noing voice mail:
Some call this a cowardly act, but if for whatever reason you just don't want to feel a push back from your no, call at 6:00 a.m. and leave it on the machine.

major no-no:
A transgression so obvious that a first grader knows not to do it. Like touching your stuff.

family no:

Reach back into your past and revisit ways your family said no. Was it effective? Was it sane? Much can be learned from history.

agent of no:

Sort of like a messenger; an angel, if you will. This person stands between you and the request and delivers the no for you. Most often, an agent of no is inextricably linked to the requester, as in a son replying to his mother's request that his wife join her gin- and French onion dip–soaked bridge game with women from her church committee.

John McCain no:

Outnumbered, alone, you must not give up any information to the enemy. You smile and quietly repeat your rank and serial number. You will not engage in combat today, for today is a family holiday gathering.

no patience:

When confronted with horrible inequities that you have no power to change, you must bide your time. Life being life, you will be confronted with something ugly that you can change. Be ready. We're counting on you.

profound no:
An act of saying no that has repercussions far beyond the moment of noing. A perfect example: moving to Canada to avoid the draft during the Vietnam War.

self-noification:
The act of putting oneself on notice that you cannot put any additional charges on your credit card bill, have any more dark chocolate bridge mix, or flirt with the neighbor guy in the driveway anymore.

personal no problem:
When confronted with strange obsessions and compulsions—mine almost always involve peanut M&M's—you must be able to tell yourself no. And mean it.

NO DISCUSSION

So you've reached the end of this little riff on no. What does it all mean? Well, nothing, if you can't put it into action. Like all things worth knowing and doing, using no takes time, thought, and practice. One person saying no can turn and help another. The power of no will grow stronger and begin to take hold. Magic will happen.

Where there is one woman, there is bound to be another, and their discussion will ultimately turn to sad stories born of their inability to say no. So you've been burned some. But why? Why couldn't you say that one wee, fun-to-form-on-the-tongue-and-lips word?

No Questions to Ask Yourself and Others

* Can you tell a story or two about a situation where the word *no* would have really saved your butt?

* Can you remember saying no and your life changed for the better?

* When you say no, is it clear to the other person that's what you're saying?

* What words or gestures, exactly, do you use to say no?

* Are there better words? Better actions to convey no?

* When you don't say yes to something you don't want to do, why are you doing it? To keep the peace? To make people happy? Did you indeed keep the peace? Did everyone get and stay happy?

* Can you say no to an authority figure?

* Can you say no to someone you are having sex with?

* Can you say no to someone you love?

* If you say a polite, respectful no, what do you think you will get in return?

* If you agree to do the thing you do not want to do, what is that going to do to your insides?

* Can you really live with being a weenie?

ACKNOWLEDGMENTS

I would like to acknowledge my late mother, Jenny, a person of no and substantial wild woman who was not beyond a good car chase if it meant keeping her daughter from an unsupervised party where there might be beer and/or boys. I would also like to thank my father, whose no was the simple statement "I'm going to Winn-Dixie" (with that, you always knew whatever was going on was over; you lose, he grocery shops), as well as my brothers, stuff touchers extraordinaire.

Many women—and men—told me about situations that screamed for the word *no,* a word they had not yet learned to speak. Their extraordinary true stories have given this book weight and a lot of funny stuff that seems unbelievable even as I type it up now.

I would also like to specially thank my muses—my girlfriends, women I have known long enough to watch graduate from making out in cars to buying their first Lexus and, at all times, who wore extraordinary shoes no matter what they were doing. They have beaten everything from cheating husbands to cancer and kept laughing. It was an honor to watch them grow up.

Finally, thanks to my fantastic designated editor at Rodale, Shannon Welch, who stepped in and landed this book with grace and wit, and David Black, my agent, who actually has a bunch of big-shot authors who shoot to the top of bestseller lists but still finds time for me.

ABOUT THE AUTHOR

BETH WAREHAM is a book editor for Scribner, a division of Simon & Schuster. She is married to her first and last husband. They recently celebrated their 10th wedding anniversary, a fact that completely baffles the both of them. They live in New York City and on an island off the coast of Canada.

INDEX

C

D

142

143

145